CLEP-40 COLLEGE-LEVEL EXAMINATION
PROGRAM SERIES

This is your
PASSBOOK for...

Principles of/ Introductory Microeconomics

Test Preparation Study Guide
Questions & Answers

COPYRIGHT NOTICE

This book is SOLELY intended for, is sold ONLY to, and its use is RESTRICTED to individual, bona fide applicants or candidates who qualify by virtue of having seriously filed applications for appropriate license, certificate, professional and/or promotional advancement, higher school matriculation, scholarship, or other legitimate requirements of education and/or governmental authorities.

This book is NOT intended for use, class instruction, tutoring, training, duplication, copying, reprinting, excerption, or adaptation, etc., by:

1) Other publishers
2) Proprietors and/or Instructors of "Coaching" and/or Preparatory Courses
3) Personnel and/or Training Divisions of commercial, industrial, and governmental organizations
4) Schools, colleges, or universities and/or their departments and staffs, including teachers and other personnel
5) Testing Agencies or Bureaus
6) Study groups which seek by the purchase of a single volume to copy and/or duplicate and/or adapt this material for use by the group as a whole without having purchased individual volumes for each of the members of the group
7) Et al.

Such persons would be in violation of appropriate Federal and State statutes.

PROVISION OF LICENSING AGREEMENTS – Recognized educational, commercial, industrial, and governmental institutions and organizations, and others legitimately engaged in educational pursuits, including training, testing, and measurement activities, may address request for a licensing agreement to the copyright owners, who will determine whether, and under what conditions, including fees and charges, the materials in this book may be used them. In other words, a licensing facility exists for the legitimate use of the material in this book on other than an individual basis. However, it is asseverated and affirmed here that the material in this book CANNOT be used without the receipt of the express permission of such a licensing agreement from the Publishers. Inquiries re licensing should be addressed to the company, attention rights and permissions department.

All rights reserved, including the right of reproduction in whole or in part, in any form or by any means, electronic or mechanical, including photocopying, recording, or by any information storage and retrieval system, without permission in writing from the Publisher.

Copyright © 2025 by
National Learning Corporation

212 Michael Drive, Syosset, NY 11791
(516) 921-8888 • www.passbooks.com
E-mail: info@passbooks.com

PASSBOOK® SERIES

THE *PASSBOOK® SERIES* has been created to prepare applicants and candidates for the ultimate academic battlefield – the examination room.

At some time in our lives, each and every one of us may be required to take an examination – for validation, matriculation, admission, qualification, registration, certification, or licensure.

Based on the assumption that every applicant or candidate has met the basic formal educational standards, has taken the required number of courses, and read the necessary texts, the *PASSBOOK® SERIES* furnishes the one special preparation which may assure passing with confidence, instead of failing with insecurity. Examination questions – together with answers – are furnished as the basic vehicle for study so that the mysteries of the examination and its compounding difficulties may be eliminated or diminished by a sure method.

This book is meant to help you pass your examination provided that you qualify and are serious in your objective.

The entire field is reviewed through the huge store of content information which is succinctly presented through a provocative and challenging approach – the question-and-answer method.

A climate of success is established by furnishing the correct answers at the end of each test.

You soon learn to recognize types of questions, forms of questions, and patterns of questioning. You may even begin to anticipate expected outcomes.

You perceive that many questions are repeated or adapted so that you can gain acute insights, which may enable you to score many sure points.

You learn how to confront new questions, or types of questions, and to attack them confidently and work out the correct answers.

You note objectives and emphases, and recognize pitfalls and dangers, so that you may make positive educational adjustments.

Moreover, you are kept fully informed in relation to new concepts, methods, practices, and directions in the field.

You discover that you are actually taking the examination all the time: you are preparing for the examination by "taking" an examination, not by reading extraneous and/or supererogatory textbooks.

In short, this PASSBOOK®, used directedly, should be an important factor in helping you to pass your test.

NONTRADITIONAL EDUCATION

Students returning to school as adults bring more varied experience to their studies than do the teenagers who begin college shortly after graduating from high school. As a result, there are numerous programs for students with nontraditional learning curves. Hundreds of colleges and universities grant degrees to people who cannot attend classes at a regular campus or have already learned what the college is supposed to teach.

You can earn nontraditional education credits in many ways:
- Passing standardized exams
- Demonstrating knowledge gained through experience
- Completing campus-based coursework, and
- Taking courses off campus

Some methods of assessing learning for credit are objective, such as standardized tests. Others are more subjective, such as a review of life experiences.

With some help from four hypothetical characters – Alice, Vin, Lynette, and Jorge – this article describes nontraditional ways of earning educational credit. It begins by describing programs in which you can earn a high school diploma without spending 4 years in a classroom. The college picture is more complicated, so it is presented in two parts: one on gaining credit for what you know through course work or experience, and a second on college degree programs. The final section lists resources for locating more information.

Earning High School Credit

People who were prevented from finishing high school as teenagers have several options if they want to do so as adults. Some major cities have back-to-school programs that allow adults to attend high school classes with current students. But the more practical alternatives for most adults are to take the General Educational Development (GED) tests or to earn a high school diploma by demonstrating their skills or taking correspondence classes.

Of course, these options do not match the experience of staying in high school and graduating with one's friends. But they are viable alternatives for adult learners committed to meeting and, often, continuing their educational goals.

GED Program

Alice quit high school her sophomore year and took a job to help support herself, her younger brother, and their newly widowed mother. Now an adult, she wants to earn her high school diploma – and then go on to college. Because her job as head cook and her family responsibilities keep her busy during the day, she plans to get a high school equivalency diploma. She will study for, and take, the GED tests. Every year, about half a million adults earn their high school credentials this way. A GED diploma is accepted in lieu of a high school one by more than 90 percent of employers, colleges, and universities, so it is a good choice for someone like Alice.

The GED testing program is sponsored by the American Council on Education and State and local education departments. It consists of examinations in five subject areas: Writing, science, mathematics, social studies, and literature and the arts. The tests also measure skills such as analytical ability, problem solving, reading comprehension, and ability to understand and apply information. Most of the questions are multiple choice; the writing test includes an essay section on a topic of general interest.

Eligibility rules for taking the exams vary, but some states require that you must be at least 18. Tests are given in English, Spanish, and French. In addition to standard print, versions in large print, Braille, and audiocassette are also available. Total time allotted for the tests is 7 1/2 hours.

The GED tests are not easy. About one-fourth of those who complete the exams every year do not pass. Passing scores are established by administering the tests to a sample of graduating high school seniors. The minimum standard score is set so that about one-third of graduating seniors would not pass the tests if they took them.

Because of the difficulty of the tests, people need to prepare themselves to take them. Often, they start by taking the Official GED Practice Tests, usually available through a local adult education center. Centers are listed in your phone book's blue pages under "Adult Education," "Continuing Education," or "GED." Adult education centers also have information about GED preparation classes and self-study materials. Classes are generally arranged to accommodate adults' work schedules. National Learning Corporation publishes several study guides that aim to thoroughly prepare test-takers for the GED.

School districts, colleges, adult education centers, and community organizations have information about GED testing schedules and practice tests. For more information, contact them, your nearest GED testing center, or:

GED Testing Service
One Dupont Circle, NW, Suite 250
Washington, DC 20036-1163
1(800) 62-MY GED (626-9433)
(202) 939-9490

Skills Demonstration

Adults who have acquired high school level skills through experience might be eligible for the National External Diploma Program. This alternative to the GED does not involve any direct instruction. Instead, adults seeking a high school diploma must demonstrate mastery of 65 competencies in 8 general areas: Communication; computation; occupational preparedness; and self, social, consumer, scientific, and technological awareness.

Mastery is shown through the completion of the tasks. For example, a participant could prove competency in computation by measuring a room for carpeting, figuring out the amount of carpet needed, and computing the cost.

Before being accepted for the program, adults undergo an evaluation. Tests taken at one of the program's offices measure reading, writing, and mathematics abilities. A take-home segment includes a self-assessment of current skills, an individual skill evaluation, and an occupational interest and aptitude test.

Adults accepted for the program have weekly meetings with an assessor. At the meeting, the assessor reviews the participant's work from the previous week. If the task has not been completed properly, the assessor explains the mistake. Participants continue to correct their errors until they master each competency. A high school diploma is awarded upon proven mastery of all 65 competencies.

Fourteen States and the District of Columbia now offer the External Diploma Program. For more information, contact:

External Diploma Program
One Dupont Circle, NW, Suite 250
Washington, DC 20036-1193
(202) 939-9475

Correspondence and Distance Study

Vin dropped out of high school during his junior year because his family's frequent moves made it difficult for him to continue his studies. He promised himself at the time he dropped out that he would someday finish the courses needed for his diploma. For people like Vin, who prefer to earn a traditional diploma in a nontraditional way, there are about a dozen accredited courses of study for earning a high school diploma by correspondence, or distance study. The programs are either privately run, affiliated with a university, or administered by a State education department.

Distance study diploma programs have no residency requirements, allowing students to continue their studies from almost any location. Depending on the course of study, students need not be enrolled full time and usually have more flexible schedules for finishing their work. Selection of courses ranges from vo-tech to college prep, and some programs place different emphasis on the types of diplomas offered. University affiliated schools, for example, allow qualified students to take college courses along with their high school ones. Students can then apply the college credits toward a degree at that university or transfer them to another institution.

Taking courses by distance study is often more challenging and time consuming than attending classes, especially for adults who have other obligations. Success depends on each student's motivation. Students usually do reading assignments on their own. Written exercises, which they complete and send to an instructor for grading, supplement their reading material.

A list of some accredited high schools that offer diplomas by distance study is available free from the Distance Education and Training Council, formerly known as the National Home Study Council. Request the "DETC Directory of Accredited Institutions" from:

The Distance Education and Training Council
1601 18th Street, NW.
Washington, DC 20009-2529
(202) 234-5100

Some publications profiling nontraditional college programs include addresses and descriptions of several high school correspondence ones. See the Resources section at the end of this article for more information.

Getting College Credit For What You Know

Adults can receive college credit for prior coursework, by passing examinations, and documenting experiential learning. With help from a college advisor, nontraditional students should assess their skills, establish their educational goals, and determine the number of college credits they might be eligible for.

Even before you meet with a college advisor, you should collect all your school and training records. Then, make a list of all knowledge and abilities acquired through experience, no matter how irrelevant they seem to your chosen field. Next, determine your educational goals: What specific field do you wish to study? What kind of a degree do you want? Finally, determine how your past work fits into the field of study. Later on, you will evaluate educational programs to find one that's right for you.

People who have complex educational or experiential learning histories might want to have their learning evaluated by the Regents Credit Bank. The Credit Bank, operated by Regents College of the University of the State of New York, allows people to consolidate credits earned through college, experience, or other methods. Special assessments are available for Regents College enrollees whose knowledge in a specific field cannot be adequately evaluated by standardized exams. For more information, contact the Regents Credit Bank at:

Regents College
7 Columbia Circle
Albany, NY 12203-5159
(518) 464-8500

Credit For Prior College Coursework

When Lynette was in college during the 1970s, she attended several different schools and took a variety of courses. She did well in some classes and poorly in others. Now that she is a successful business owner and has more focus, Lynette thinks she should forget about her previous coursework and start from scratch. Instead, she should start from where she is.

Lynette should have all her transcripts sent to the colleges or universities of her choice and let an admissions officer determine which classes are applicable toward a degree. A few credits here and there may not seem like much, but they add up. Even if the subjects do not seem relevant to any major, they might be counted as elective credits toward a degree. And comparing the cost of transcripts with the cost of college courses, it makes sense to spend a few dollars per transcript for a chance to save hundreds, and perhaps thousands, of dollars in books and tuition.

Rules for transferring credits apply to all prior coursework at accredited colleges and universities, whether done on campus or off. Courses completed off campus, often called extended learning, include those available to students through independent study and correspondence. Many schools have extended learning programs; Brigham Young University, for example, offers more than 300 courses through its Department of Independent Study. One type of extended learning is distance learning, a form of correspondence study by technological means such as television, video and audio, CD-ROM, electronic mail, and computer tutorials. See the Resources section at the end of this article for more information about publications available from the National University Continuing Education Association.

Any previously earned college credits should be considered for transfer, no matter what the subject or the grade received. Many schools do not accept the transfer of courses graded below a C or ones taken more than a designated number of years ago. Some colleges and universities also have limits on the number of credits that can be transferred and applied toward a degree. But not all do. For example, Thomas Edison State College, New Jersey's State college for adults, accepts the transfer of all 120 hours of credit required for a baccalaureate degree – provided all the credits are transferred from regionally accredited schools, no more than 80 are at the junior college level, and the student's grades overall and in the field of study average out to C.

To assign credit for prior coursework, most schools require original transcripts. This means you must complete a form or send a written, signed request to have your transcripts released directly to a college or university. Once you have chosen the schools you want to apply to, contact the schools you attended before. Find out how much each transcript costs, and ask them to send your transcripts to the ones you are applying to. Write a letter that includes your name (and names used during attendance, if different) and dates of attendance, along with the names and addresses of the schools to which your transcripts should be sent. Include payment and mail to the registrar at the schools you have attended. The registrar's office will process your request and send an official transcript of your coursework to the colleges or universities you have designated.

Credit For Noncollege Courses

Colleges and universities are not the only ones that offer classes. Volunteer organizations and employers often provide formal training worth college credit. The American Council on Education has two programs that assess thousands of specific courses and make recommendations on the amount of college credit they are worth. Colleges and universities accept the recommendations or use them as guidelines.

One program evaluates educational courses sponsored by government agencies, business and industry, labor unions, and professional and voluntary organizations. It is the Program on Noncollegiate Sponsored Instruction (PONSI). Some of the training seminars Alice has participated in covered topics such as food preparation, kitchen safety, and nutrition. Although she has not yet earned her GED, Alice can earn college credit because of her completion of these formal job-training seminars. The number of credits each seminar is worth does not hinge on Alice's current eligibility for college enrollment.

The other program evaluates courses offered by the Army, Navy, Air Force, Marines, Coast Guard, and Department of Defense. It is the Military Evaluations Program. Jorge has never attended college, but the engineering technology classes he completed as part of his military training are worth college credit. And as an Army veteran, Jorge is eligible for a service that takes the evaluations one step further. The Army/American Council on Education Registry Transcript System (AARTS) will provide Jorge with an individualized transcript of American Council on Education credit recommendations for all courses he completed, the military occupational specialties (MOS's) he held, and examinations he passed while in the Army. All Army and National Guard enlisted personnel and veterans who enlisted after October 1981 are eligible for the transcript. Similar services are being considered by the Navy and Marine Corps.

To obtain a free transcript, see your Army Education Center for a 5454R transcript request form. Include your name, Social Security number, basic active service date, and complete address where you want the transcript sent. Mail your request to:

AARTS Operations Center
415 McPherson Ave.
Fort Leavenworth, KS 66027-1373

Recommendations for PONSI are published in *The National Guide to Educational Credit for Training Programs;* military program recommendations are in *The Guide to the Evaluation of Educational Experiences in the Armed Forces.* See the Resources section at the end of this article for more information about these publications.

Former military personnel who took a foreign language course through the Defense Language Institute may request course transcripts by sending their name, Social Security number, course title, duration of the course, and graduation date to:

    Commandant, Defense Language Institute
    Attn: ATFL-DAA-AR
    Transcripts
    Presidio of Monterey
    Monterey, CA 93944-5006

Not all of Jorge's and Alice's courses have been assessed by the American Council on Education. Training courses that have no Council credit recommendation should still be assessed by an advisor at the schools they want to attend. Course descriptions, class notes, test scores, and other documentation may be helpful for comparing training courses to their college equivalents. An oral examination or other demonstration of competency might also be required.

There is no guarantee you will receive all the credits you are seeking – but you certainly won't if you make no attempt.

Credit By Examination

Standardized tests are the best-known method of receiving college credit without taking courses. These exams are often taken by high school students seeking advanced placement for college, but they are also available to adult learners. Testing programs and colleges and universities offer exams in a number of subjects. Two U.S. Government institutes have foreign language exams for employees that also may be worth college credit.

It is important to understand that receiving a passing score on these exams does not mean you get college credit automatically. Each school determines which test results it will accept, minimum scores required, how scores are converted for credit, and the amount of credit, if any, to be assigned. Most colleges and universities accept the American Council on Education credit recommendations, published every other year in the 250-page *Guide to Educational Credit by Examination*. For more information, contact:

    The American Council on Education
    Credit by Examination Program
    One Dupont Circle, Suite 250
    Washington, DC 20036-1193
    (202) 939-9434

Testing programs:

You might know some of the five national testing programs by their acronyms or initials: CLEP, ACT PEP: RCE, DANTES, AP, and NOCTI. (The meanings of these initialisms are explained below.) There is some overlap among programs; for example, four of them have introductory accounting exams. Since you will not be awarded credit more than once for a specific subject, you should carefully evaluate each program for the subject exams you wish to take. And before taking an exam, make sure you will be awarded credit by the college or university you plan to attend.

CLEP (College-Level Examination Program), administered by the College Board, is the most widely accepted of the national testing programs; more than 2,800 accredited schools award credit for passing exam scores. Each test covers material taught in basic undergraduate courses. There are five general exams – English composition, humanities, college mathematics, natural sciences, and social sciences and history – and many subject exams. Most exams are entirely multiple-choice, but English composition exams may include an essay section. For more information, contact:

    CLEP
    P.O. Box 6600
    Princeton, NJ 08541-6600
    (609) 771-7865

ACT PEP: RCE (American College Testing Proficiency Exam Program: Regents College Examinations) tests are given in 38 subjects within arts and sciences, business, education, and nursing. Each exam is recommended for either lower- or upper-level credit. Exams contain either objective or extended response questions, and are graded according to a standard score, letter grade, or pass/fail. Fees vary, depending on the subject and type of exam. For more information or to request free study guides, contact:

    ACT PEP: Regents College Examinations
    P.O. Box 4014
    Iowa City, IA 52243
    (319) 337-1387
    (New York State residents must contact Regents College directly.)

DANTES (Defense Activity for Nontraditional Education Support) standardized tests are developed by the Educational Testing Service for the Department of Defense. Originally administered only to military personnel, the exams have been available to the public since 1983. About 50 subject tests cover business, mathematics, social science, physical science, humanities, foreign languages, and applied technology. Most of the tests consist entirely of multiple-choice questions. Schools determine their own administering fees and testing schedules. For more information or to request free study sheets, contact:

    DANTES Program Office
    Mail Stop 31-X
    Educational Testing Service
    Princeton, NJ 08541
    1(800) 257-9484

The AP (Advanced Placement) Program is a cooperative effort between secondary schools and colleges and universities. AP exams are developed each year by committees of college and high school faculty appointed by the College Board and assisted by consultants from the Educational Testing Service. Subjects include arts and languages, natural sciences, computer science, social sciences, history, and mathematics. Most tests are 2 or 3 hours long and include both multiple-choice and essay questions. AP courses are available to help students prepare for exams, which are offered in the spring. For more information about the Advanced Placement Program, contact:

    Advanced Placement Services
    P.O. Box 6671
    Princeton, NJ 08541-6671
    (609) 771-7300

NOCTI (National Occupational Competency Testing Institute) assessments are designed for people like Alice, who have vocational-technical skills that cannot be evaluated by other tests. NOCTI assesses competency at two levels: Student/job ready and teacher/experienced worker. Standardized evaluations are available for occupations such as auto-body repair, electronics, mechanical drafting, quantity food preparation, and upholstering. The tests consist of multiple-choice questions and a performance component. Other services include workshops, customized assessments, and pre-testing. For more information, contact:

NOCTI
500 N. Bronson Ave.
Ferris State University
Big Rapids, MI 49307
(616) 796-4699

Colleges and universities:

Many colleges and universities have credit-by-exam programs, through which students earn credit by passing a comprehensive exam for a course offered by the institution. Among the most widely recognized are the programs at Ohio University, the University of North Carolina, Thomas Edison State College, and New York University.

Ohio University offers about 150 examinations for credit. In addition, you may sometimes arrange to take special examinations in non-laboratory courses offered at Ohio University. To take a test for credit, you must enroll in the course. If you plan to transfer the credit earned, you also need written permission from an official at your school. Books and study materials are available, for a cost, through the university. Exams must be taken within 6 months of the enrollment date; most last 3 hours. You may arrange to take the exam off campus if you do not live near the university.

Ohio University is on the quarter-hour system; most courses are worth 4 quarter hours, the equivalent of 3 semester hours. For more information, contact:

Independent Study
Tupper Hall 302
Ohio University
Athens, OH 45701-2979
1(800) 444-2910
(614) 593-2910

The University of North Carolina offers a credit-by-examination option for 140 independent study (correspondence) courses in foreign languages, humanities, social sciences, mathematics, business administration, education, electrical and computer engineering, health administration, and natural sciences. To take an exam, you must request and receive approval from both the course instructor and the independent studies department. Exams must be taken within six months of enrollment, and you may register for no more than two at a time. If you are not near the University's Chapel Hill campus, you may take your exam under supervision at an accredited college, university, community college, or technical institute. For more information, contact:

Independent Studies
CB #1020, The Friday Center
UNC-Chapel Hill
Chapel Hill, NC 27599-1020
1(800) 862-5669 / (919) 962-1134

The Thomas Edison College Examination Program offers more than 50 exams in liberal arts, business, and professional areas. Thomas Edison State College administers tests twice a month in Trenton, New Jersey; however, students may arrange to take their tests with a proctor at any accredited American college or university or U.S. military base. Most of the tests are multiple choice; some also include short answer or essay questions. Time limits range from 90 minutes to 4 hours, depending on the exam. For more information, contact:

Thomas Edison State College
TECEP, Office of Testing and Assessment
101 W. State Street
Trenton, NJ 08608-1176
(609) 633-2844

New York University's Foreign Language Program offers proficiency exams in more than 40 languages, from Albanian to Yiddish. Two exams are available in each language: The 12-point test is equivalent to 4 undergraduate semesters, and the 16-point exam may lead to upper level credit. The tests are given at the university's Foreign Language Department throughout the year.

Proof of foreign language proficiency does not guarantee college credit. Some colleges and universities accept transcripts only for languages commonly taught, such as French and Spanish. Nontraditional programs are more likely than traditional ones to grant credit for proficiency in other languages.

For an informational brochure and registration form for NYU's foreign language proficiency exams, contact:

New York University
Foreign Language Department
48 Cooper Square, Room 107
New York, NY 10003
(212) 998-7030

Government institutes:

The Defense Language Institute and Foreign Service Institute administer foreign language proficiency exams for personnel stationed abroad. Usually, the tests are given at the end of intensive language courses or upon completion of service overseas. But some people – like Jorge, who knows Spanish – speak another language fluently and may be allowed to take a proficiency exam in that language before completing their tour of duty. Contact one of the offices listed below to obtain transcripts of those scores. Proof of proficiency does not guarantee college credit, however, as discussed above.

To request score reports from the Defense Language Institute for Defense Language Proficiency Tests, send your name, Social Security number, language for which you were tested, and, most importantly, when and where you took the exam to:

Commandant, Defense Language Institute
Attn: ATFL-ES-T
DLPT Score Report Request
Presidio of Monterey
Monterey, CA 93944-5006

To request transcripts of scores for Foreign Service Institute exams, send your name, Social Security number, language for which you were tested, and dates or year of exams to:

Foreign Service Institute
Arlington Hall
4020 Arlington Boulevard
Rosslyn, VA 22204-1500
Attn: Testing Office (Send your request to the attention of the testing office of the foreign language in which you were tested)

Credit For Experience

Experiential learning credit may be given for knowledge gained through job responsibilities, personal hobbies, volunteer opportunities, homemaking, and other experiences. Colleges and universities base credit awards on the knowledge you have attained, not for the experience alone. In addition, the knowledge must be college level; not just any learning will do. Throwing horseshoes as a hobby is not likely to be worth college credit. But if you've done research on how and where the sport originated, visited blacksmiths, organized tournaments, and written a column for a trade journal – well, that's a horseshoe of a different color.

Adults attempting to get credit for their experience should be forewarned: Having your experience evaluated for college credit is time-consuming, tedious work – not an easy shortcut for people who want quick-fix college credits. And not all experience, no matter how valuable, is the equivalent of college courses.

Requesting college credit for your experiential learning can be tricky. You should get assistance from a credit evaluations officer at the school you plan to attend, but you should also have a general idea of what your knowledge is worth. A common method for converting knowledge into credit is to use a college catalog. Find course titles and descriptions that match what you have learned through experience, and request the number of credits offered for those courses.

Once you know what credit to ask for, you must usually present your case in writing to officials at the college you plan to attend. The most common form of presenting experiential learning for credit is the portfolio. A portfolio is a written record of your knowledge along with a request for equivalent college credit. It includes an identification and description of the knowledge for which you are requesting credit, an explanatory essay of how the knowledge was gained and how it fits into your educational plans, documentation that you have acquired such knowledge, and a request for college credit. Required elements of a portfolio vary by schools but generally follow those guidelines.

In identifying knowledge you have gained, be specific about exactly what you have learned. For example, it is not enough for Lynette to say she runs a business. She must identify the knowledge she has gained from running it, such as personnel management, tax law, marketing strategy, and inventory review. She must also include brief descriptions about her knowledge of each to support her claims of having those skills.

The essay gives you a chance to relay something about who you are. It should address your educational goals, include relevant autobiographical details, and be well organized, neat, and convey confidence. In his essay, Jorge might first state his goal of becoming an engineer. Then he would explain why he joined the Army, where he got hands-on training and experience in developing and servicing electronic equipment.

This, he would say, led to his hobby of creating remote-controlled model cars, of which he has built 20. His conclusion would highlight his accomplishments and tie them to his desire to become an electronic engineer.

Documentation is evidence that you've learned what you claim to have learned. You can show proof of knowledge in a variety of ways, including audio or video recordings, letters from current or former employers describing your specific duties and job performance, blueprints, photographs or artwork, and transcripts of certifying exams for professional licenses and certification – such as Alice's certification from the American Culinary Federation. Although documentation can take many forms, written proof alone is not always enough. If it is impossible to document your knowledge in writing, find out if your experiential learning can be assessed through supplemental oral exams by a faculty expert.

Earning a College Degree

Nontraditional students often have work, family, and financial obligations that prevent them from quitting their jobs to attend school full time. Can they still meet their educational goals? Yes.

More than 150 accredited colleges and universities have nontraditional bachelor's degree programs that require students to spend little or no time on campus; over 300 others have nontraditional campus-based degree programs. Some of those schools, as well as most junior and community colleges, offer associate's degrees nontraditionally. Each school with a nontraditional course of study determines its own rules for awarding credit for prior coursework, exams, or experience, as discussed previously. Most have charges on top of tuition for providing these special services.

Several publications profile nontraditional degree programs; see the Resources section at the end of this article for more information. To determine which school best fits your academic profile and educational goals, first list your criteria. Then, evaluate nontraditional programs based on their accreditation, features, residency requirements, and expenses. Once you have chosen several schools to explore further, write to them for more information. Detailed explanations of school policies should help you decide which ones you want to apply to.

Get beyond the printed word – especially the glowing words each school writes about itself. Check out the schools you are considering with higher education authorities, alumni, employers, family members, and friends. If possible, visit the campus to talk to students and instructors and sit in on a few classes, even if you will be completing most or all of your work off campus. Ask school officials questions about such things as enrollment numbers, graduation rate, faculty qualifications, and confusing details about the application process or academic policies. After you have thoroughly investigated each prospective college or university, you can make an informed decision about which is right for you.

Accreditation

Accreditation is a process colleges and universities submit to voluntarily for getting their credentials. An accredited school has been investigated and visited by teams of observers and has periodic inspections by a private accrediting agency. The initial review can take two years or more.

Regional agencies accredit entire schools, and professional agencies accredit either specialized schools or departments within schools. Although there are no national accrediting standards, not just any accreditation will do. Countless "accreditation associations" have been invented by schools, many of which have no academic programs and sell phony degrees, to accredit themselves. But 6 regional and about 80 professional accrediting associations in the United States are recognized by the U.S. Department of Education or the Commission on Recognition of Postsecondary Accreditation. When checking accreditation, these are the names to look for. For more information about accreditation and accrediting agencies, contact:

>Institutional Participation Oversight Service Accreditation and State Liaison Division
>U.S. Department of Education
>ROB 3, Room 3915
>600 Independence Ave., SW
>Washington, DC 20202-5244
>(202) 708-7417

Because accreditation is not mandatory, lack of accreditation does not necessarily mean a school or program is bad. Some schools choose not to apply for accreditation, are in the process of applying, or have educational methods too unconventional for an accrediting association's standards. For the nontraditional student, however, earning a degree from a college or university with recognized accreditation is an especially important consideration. Although nontraditional education is becoming more widely accepted, it is not yet mainstream. Employers skeptical of a degree earned in a nontraditional manner are likely to be even less accepting of one from an unaccredited school.

Program Features

Because nontraditional students have diverse educational objectives, nontraditional schools are diverse in what they offer. Some programs are geared toward helping students organize their scattered educational credits to get a degree as quickly as possible. Others cater to those who may have specific credits or experience but need assistance in completing requirements. Whatever your educational profile, you should look for a program that works with you in obtaining your educational goals.

A few nontraditional programs have special admissions policies for adult learners like Alice, who plan to earn their GEDs but want to enroll in college in the meantime. Other features of nontraditional programs include individualized learning agreements, intensive academic counseling, cooperative learning and internship placement, and waiver of some prerequisites or other requirements – as well as college credit for prior coursework, examinations, and experiential learning, all discussed previously.

Lynette, whose primary goal is to finish her degree, wants to earn maximum credits for her business experience. She will look for programs that do not limit the number of credits awarded for equivalency exams and experiential learning. And since well-documented proof of knowledge is essential for earning experiential learning credits, Lynette should make sure the program she chooses provides assistance to students submitting a portfolio.

Jorge, on the other hand, has more credits than he needs in certain areas and is willing to forego some. To become an engineer, he must have a bachelor's degree; but because he is accustomed to hands-on learning, Jorge is interested in getting experience as he gains more technical skills. He will concentrate on finding schools with strong cooperative education, supervised fieldwork, or internship programs.

Residency Requirements

Programs are sometimes deemed nontraditional because of their residency requirements. Many people think of residency for colleges and universities in terms of tuition, with in-state students paying less than out-of-state ones. Residency also may refer to where a student lives, either on or off campus, while attending school.

But in nontraditional education, residency usually refers to how much time students must spend on campus, regardless of whether they attend classes there. In some nontraditional programs, students need not ever step foot on campus. Others require only a very short residency, such as one day or a few weeks. Many schools have standard residency requirements of several semesters but schedule classes for evenings or weekends to accommodate working adults.

Lynette, who previously took courses by independent study, prefers to earn credits by distance study. She will focus on schools that have no residency requirement. Several colleges and universities have nonresident degree completion programs for adults with some college credit. Under the direction of a faculty advisor, students devise a plan for earning their remaining credits. Methods for earning credits include independent study, distance learning, seminars, supervised fieldwork, and group study at arranged sites. Students may have to earn a certain number of credits through the degree-granting institution. But many programs allow students to take courses at accredited schools of their choice for transfer toward their degree.

Alice wants to attend lectures but has an unpredictable schedule. Her best course of action will be to seek out short residency programs that require students to attend seminars once or twice a semester. She can take courses that are televised and videotape them to watch when her schedule permits, with the seminars helping to ensure that she properly completes her coursework. Many colleges and universities with short residency requirements also permit students to earn some credits elsewhere, by whatever means the student chooses.

Some fields of study require classroom instruction. As Jorge will discover, few colleges and universities allow students to earn a bachelor's degree in engineering entirely through independent study. Nontraditional residency programs are designed to accommodate adults' daytime work schedules. Jorge should look for programs offering evening, weekend, summer, and accelerated courses.

Tuition and Other Expenses

The final decisions about which schools Alice, Jorge, and Lynette attend may hinge in large part on a single issue: Cost. And rising tuition is only part of the equation. Beginning with application fees and continuing through graduation fees, college expenses add up.

Traditional and nontraditional students have some expenses in common, such as the cost of books and other materials. Tuition might even be the same for some courses, especially for colleges and universities offering standard ones at unusual times. But for nontraditional programs, students may also pay fees for services such as credit or transcript review, evaluation, advisement, and portfolio assessment.

Students are also responsible for postage and handling or setup expenses for independent study courses, as well as for all examination and transcript fees for transferring credits. Usually, the more nontraditional the program, the more detailed the fees. Some schools charge a yearly enrollment fee rather than tuition for degree completion candidates who want their files to remain active.

Although tuition and fees might seem expensive, most educators tell you not to let money come between you and your educational goals. Talk to someone in the financial aid department of the school you plan to attend or check your library for publications about financial aid sources. The U.S. Department of Education publishes a guide to Federal aid programs such as Pell Grants, student loans, and work-study. To order the free 74-page booklet, *The Student Guide: Financial Aid from the U.S. Department of Education,* contact:

Federal Student Aid Information Center
P.O. Box 84
Washington, DC 20044
1 (800) 4FED-AID (433-3243)

Resources

Information on how to earn a high school diploma or college degree without following the usual routes is available from several organizations and in numerous publications. Information on nontraditional graduate degree programs, available for master's through doctoral level, though not discussed in this article, can usually be obtained from the same resources that detail bachelor's degree programs.

National Learning Corporation publishes study guides for all of these exams, for both general examinations and tests in specific subject areas. To order study guides, or to browse their catalog featuring more than 5,000 titles, visit NLC online at www.passbooks.com, or contact them by phone at (800) 632-8888.

Organizations

Adult learners should always contact their local school system, community college, or university to learn about programs that are readily available. The following national organizations can also supply information:

American Council on Education
One Dupont Circle
Washington, DC 20036-1193
(202) 939-9300

Within the American Council on Education, the Center for Adult Learning and Educational Credentials administers the National External Diploma Program, the GED Program, the Program on Noncollegiate Sponsored Instruction, the Credit by Examination Program, and the Military Evaluations Program.

College-Level Examination Program (CLEP)

1. WHAT IS CLEP?

CLEP stands for the College-Level Examination Program, sponsored by the College Board. It is a national program of credit-by-examination that offers you the opportunity to obtain recognition for college-level achievement. No matter when, where, or how you have learned – by means of formal or informal study – you can take CLEP tests. If the results are acceptable to your college, you can receive credit.

You may not realize it, but you probably know more than your academic record reveals. Each day you, like most people, have an opportunity to learn. In private industry and business, as well as at all levels of government, learning opportunities continually occur. If you read widely or intensively in a particular field, think about what you read, discuss it with your family and friends, you are learning. Or you may be learning on a more formal basis by taking a correspondence course, a television or radio course, a course recorded on tape or cassettes, a course assembled into programmed tests, or a course taught in your community adult school or high school.

No matter how, where, or when you gained your knowledge, you may have the opportunity to receive academic credit for your achievement that can be counted toward an undergraduate degree. The College-Level Examination Program (CLEP) enables colleges to evaluate your achievement and give you credit. A wide range of college-level examinations are offered by CLEP to anyone who wishes to take them. Scores on the tests are reported to you and, if you wish, to a college, employer, or individual.

2. WHAT ARE THE PURPOSES OF THE COLLEGE-LEVEL EXAMINATION PROGRAM?

The basic purpose of the College-Level Examination Program is to enable individuals who have acquired their education in nontraditional ways to demonstrate their academic achievement. It is also intended for use by those in higher education, business, industry, government, and other fields who need a reliable method of assessing a person's educational level.

Recognizing that the real issue is not how a person has acquired his education but what education he has, the College Level Examination Program has been designed to serve a variety of purposes. The basic purpose, as listed above, is to enable those who have reached the college level of education in nontraditional ways to assess the level of their achievement and to use the test results in seeking college credit or placement.

In addition, scores on the tests can be used to validate educational experience obtained at a nonaccredited institution or through noncredit college courses.

Some colleges and universities may use the tests to measure the level of educational achievement of their students, and for various institutional research purposes.

Other colleges and universities may wish to use the tests in the admission, placement, and guidance of students who wish to transfer from one institution to another.

Businesses, industries, governmental agencies, and professional groups now accept the results of these tests as a basis for advancement, eligibility for further training, or professional or semi-professional certification.

Many people are interested in the examination simply to assess their own educational progress and attainment.

The college, university, business, industry, or government agency that adopts the tests in the College-Level Examination Program makes its own decision about how it will use and interpret the test scores. The College Board will provide the tests, score them, and report the results either to the individuals who took the tests or the college or agency that administered them. It does NOT, and cannot, award college credit, certify college equivalency, or make recommendations regarding the standards these institutions should establish for the use of the test results.

Therefore, if you are taking the tests to secure credit from an institution, you should FIRST ascertain whether the college or agency involved will accept the scores. Each institution determines which CLEP tests it will accept for credit and the amount of credit it will award. If you want to take tests for college credit, first call, write, or visit the college you wish to attend to inquire about its policy on CLEP scores, as well as its other admission requirements.

The services of the program are also available to people who have been requested to take the tests by an employer, a professional licensing agency, a certifying agency, or by other groups that recognize college equivalency on the basis of satisfactory CLEP scores. You may, of course, take the tests SOLELY for your own information. If you do, your scores will be reported only to you.

While neither CLEP nor the College Board can evaluate previous credentials or award college credit, you will receive, with your scores, basic information to help you interpret your performance on the tests you have taken.

3. WHAT ARE THE COLLEGE-LEVEL EXAMINATIONS?

In order to meet different kinds of curricular organization and testing needs at colleges and universities, the College-Level Examination Program offers 35 different subject tests falling under five separate general categories: Composition and Literature, Foreign Languages, History and Social Sciences, Science and Mathematics, and Business.

4. WHAT ARE THE SUBJECT EXAMINATIONS?

The 35 CLEP tests offered by the College Board are listed below:

COMPOSITION AND LITERATURE:
- American Literature
- Analyzing and Interpreting Literature
- English Composition
- English Composition with Essay
- English Literature
- Freshman College Composition
- Humanities

FOREIGN LANGUAGES
- French
- German
- Spanish

HISTORY AND SOCIAL SCIENCES
- American Government
- Introduction to Educational Psychology
- History of the United States I: Early Colonization to 1877
- History of the United States II: 1865 to the Present
- Human Growth and Development
- Principles of Macroeconomics
- Principles of Microeconomics
- Introductory Psychology
- Social Sciences and History
- Introductory Sociology
- Western Civilization I: Ancient Near East to 1648
- Western Civilization II: 1648 to the Present

SCIENCE AND MATHEMATICS
- College Algebra
- College Algebra-Trigonometry
- Biology
- Calculus
- Chemistry
- College Mathematics
- Natural Sciences
- Trigonometry
- Precalculus

BUSINESS
- Financial Accounting
- Introductory Business Law
- Information Systems and Computer Applications
- Principles of Management
- Principles of Marketing

CLEP Examinations cover material taught in courses that most students take as requirements in the first two years of college. A college usually grants the same amount of credit to students earning satisfactory scores on the CLEP examination as it grants to students successfully completing the equivalent course.

Many examinations are designed to correspond to one-semester courses; some, however, correspond to full-year or two-year courses.

Each exam is 90 minutes long and, except for English Composition with Essay, is made up primarily of multiple-choice questions. Some tests have several other types of questions besides multiple choice. To see a more detailed description of a particular CLEP exam, visit www.collegeboard.com/clep.

The English Composition with Essay exam is the only exam that includes a required essay. This essay is scored by college English faculty designated by CLEP and does not require an additional fee. However, other Composition and Literature tests offer optional essays, which some college and universities require and some do not. These essays are graded by faculty at the individual institutions that require them and require an additional $10 fee. Contact the particular institution to ask about essay requirements, and check with your test center for further details.

All 35 CLEP examinations are administered on computer. If you are unfamiliar with taking a test on a computer, consult the CLEP Sampler online at www.collegeboard.com/clep. The Sampler contains the same tutorials as the actual exams and helps familiarize you with navigation and how to answer different types of questions.

Points are not deducted for wrong or skipped answers – you receive one point for every correct answer. Therefore it is best that an answer is supplied for each exam question, whether it is a guess or not. The number of correct answers is then converted to a formula score. This formula, or "scaled," score is determined by a statistical process called *equating*, which adjusts for slight differences in difficulty between test forms and ensures that your score does not depend on the specific test form you took or how well others did on the same form. The scaled scores range from 20 to 80 – this is the number that will appear on your score report.

To ensure that you complete all questions in the time allotted, you would probably be wise to skip the more difficult or perplexing questions and return to them later. Although the multiple-choice items in these tests are carefully designed so as not to be tricky, misleading, or ambiguous, on the other hand, they are not all direct questions of factual information. They attempt, in their way, to elicit a response that indicates your knowledge or lack of knowledge of the material in question or your ability or inability to use or interpret a fact or idea. Thus, you should concentrate on answering the questions as they appear to be without attempting to out-guess the testmakers.

5. WHAT ARE THE FEES?

The fee for all CLEP examinations is $55. Optional essays required by some institutions are an additional $10.

6. WHEN ARE THE TESTS GIVEN?

CLEP tests are administered year-round. Consult the CLEP website (www.collegeboard.com/clep) and individual test centers for specific information.

7. WHERE ARE THE TESTS GIVEN?

More than 1,300 test centers are located on college and university campuses throughout the country, and additional centers are being established to meet increased needs. Any accredited collegiate institution with an explicit and publicly available policy of credit by examination can become a CLEP test center. To obtain a list of these centers, visit the CLEP website at www.collegeboard.com/clep.

8. HOW DO I REGISTER FOR THE COLLEGE-LEVEL EXAMINATION PROGRAM?

Contact an individual test center for information regarding registration, scheduling and fees. Registration/admission forms can also be obtained on the CLEP website.

9. MAY I REPEAT THE COLLEGE-LEVEL EXAMINATIONS?

You may repeat any examination providing at least six months have passed since you were last administered this test. If you repeat a test within a period of time less than six months, your scores will be cancelled and your fees forfeited. To repeat a test, check the appropriate space on the registration form.

10. WHEN MAY I EXPECT MY SCORE REPORTS?

With the exception of the English Composition with Essay exam, you should receive your score report instantly once the test is complete.

11. HOW SHOULD I PREPARE FOR THE COLLEGE-LEVEL EXAMINATIONS?

This book has been specifically designed to prepare candidates for these examinations. It will help you to consider, study, and review important content, principles, practices, procedures, problems, and techniques in the form of varied and concrete applications.

12. QUESTIONS AND ANSWERS APPEARING IN THIS PUBLICATION

The College-Level Examinations are offered by the College Board. Since copies of past examinations have not been made available, we have used equivalent materials, including questions and answers, which are highly recommended by us as an appropriate means of preparing for these examinations.

If you need additional information about CLEP Examinations, visit www.collegeboard.com/clep.

THE COLLEGE-LEVEL EXAMINATION PROGRAM

How The Program Works

CLEP examinations are administered at many colleges and universities across the country, and most institutions award college credit to those who do well on them. The examinations provide people who have acquired knowledge outside the usual educational settings the opportunity to show that they have learned college-level material without taking certain college courses.

The CLEP examinations cover material that is taught in introductory-level courses at many colleges and universities. Faculties at individual colleges review the tests to ensure that they cover the important material taught in their courses. Colleges differ in the examinations they accept; some colleges accept only two or three of the examinations while others accept nearly all of them.

Although CLEP is sponsored by the College Board and the examinations are scored by Educational Testing Service (ETS), neither of these organizations can award college credit. Only accredited colleges may grant credit toward a degree. When you take a CLEP examination, you may request that a copy of your score report be sent to the college you are attending or plan to attend. After evaluating your scores, the college will decide whether or not to award you credit for a certain course or courses, or to exempt you from them. If the college gives you credit, it will record the number of credits on your permanent record, thereby indicating that you have completed work equivalent to a course in that subject. If the college decides to grant exemption without giving you credit for a course, you will be permitted to omit a course that would normally be required of you and to take a course of your choice instead.

What the Examinations Are Like

The examinations consist mostly of multiple-choice questions to be answered within a 90-minute time limit. Additional information about each CLEP examination is given in the examination guide and on the CLEP website.

Where To Take the Examinations

CLEP examinations are administered throughout the year at the test centers of approximately 1,300 colleges and universities. On the CLEP website, you will find a list of institutions that award credit for satisfactory scores on CLEP examinations. Some colleges administer CLEP examinations to their own students only. Other institutions administer the tests to anyone who registers to take them. If your college does not administer the tests, contact the test centers in your area for information about its testing schedule.

Once you have been tested, your score report will be available instantly. CLEP scores are kept on file at ETS for 20 years; and during this period, for a small fee, you may have your transcript sent to another college or to anyone else you specify. (Your scores will never be sent to anyone without your approval.)

APPROACHING A COLLEGE ABOUT CLEP

The following sections provide a step-by-step approach to learning about the CLEP policy at a particular college or university. The person or office that can best assist students desiring CLEP credit may have a different title at each institution, but the following guidelines will lead you to information about CLEP at any institution.

Adults returning to college often benefit from special assistance when they approach a college. Opportunities for adults to return to formal learning in the classroom are now widespread, and colleges and universities have worked hard to make this a smooth process for older students. Many colleges have established special service offices that are staffed with trained professionals who understand the kinds of problems facing adults returning to college. If you think you might benefit from such assistance, be sure to find out whether these services are available at your college.

How to Apply for College Credit

STEP 1. Obtain the General Information Catalog and a copy of the CLEP policy from the colleges you are considering. If you have not yet applied for admission, ask for an admissions application form too.

Information about admissions and CLEP policies can be obtained by contacting college admissions offices or finding admissions information on the school websites. Tell the admissions officer that you are a prospective student and that you are interested in applying for admission and CLEP credit. Ask for a copy of the publication in which the college's complete CLEP policy is explained. Also get the name and the telephone number of the person to contact in case you have further questions about CLEP.

At this step, you may wish to obtain information from external degree colleges. Many adults find that such colleges suit their needs exceptionally well.

STEP 2. If you have not already been admitted to the college you are considering, look at its admission requirements for undergraduate students to see if you can qualify.

This is an important step because if you can't get into college, you can't get college credit for CLEP. Nearly all colleges require students to be admitted and to enroll in one or more courses before granting the students CLEP credit.

Virtually all public community colleges and a number of four-year state colleges have open admission policies for in-state students. This usually means that they admit anyone who has graduated from high school or has earned a high school equivalency diploma.

If you think you do not meet the admission requirements, contact the admissions office for an interview with a counselor. Colleges do sometimes make exceptions, particularly for adult applicants. State why you want the interview and ask what documents you should bring with you or send in advance. (These materials may include a high school transcript, transcript of previous college work, completed application for admission, etc.) Make an extra effort to have all the information requested in time for the interview.

During the interview, relax and be yourself. Be prepared to state honestly why you think you are ready and able to do college work. If you have already taken CLEP examinations and scored high enough to earn credit, you have shown that you are able to do college work. Mention this achievement to the admissions counselor because it may increase your chances of being accepted. If you have not taken a CLEP examination, you can still improve your chances of being accepted by describing how your job training or independent study has helped prepare you for college-level work. Tell the counselor what you have learned from your work and personal experiences.

STEP 3. Evaluate the college's CLEP policy.

Typically, a college lists all its academic policies, including CLEP policies, in its general catalog. You will probably find the CLEP policy statement under a heading such as Credit-by-Examination, Advanced Standing, Advanced Placement, or External Degree Program. These sections can usually be found in the front of the catalog.

Many colleges publish their credit-by-examination policies in a separate brochure, which is distributed through the campus testing office, counseling center, admissions office, or registrar's office. If you find a very general policy statement in the college catalog, seek clarification from one of these offices.

Review the material in the section of this guide entitled Questions to Ask About a College's CLEP Policy. Use these guidelines to evaluate the college's CLEP policy. If you have not yet taken a CLEP examination, this evaluation will help you decide which examinations to take and whether or not to take the free-response or essay portion. Because individual colleges have different CLEP policies, a review of several policies may help you decide which college to attend.

STEP 4. If you have not yet applied for admission, do so early.

Most colleges expect you to apply for admission several months before you enroll, and it is essential that you meet the published application deadlines. It takes time to process your application for admission; and if you have yet to take a CLEP examination, it will be some time before the college receives and reviews your score report. You will probably want to take some, if not all, of the CLEP examinations you are interested in before you enroll so you know which courses you need not register for. In fact, some colleges require that all CLEP scores be submitted before a student registers.

Complete all forms and include all documents requested with your application(s) for admission. Normally, an admissions decision cannot be reached until all documents have been submitted and evaluated. Unless told to do so, do not send your CLEP scores until you have been officially admitted.

STEP 5. Arrange to take CLEP examination(s) or to submit your CLEP score(s).

You may want to wait to take your CLEP examinations until you know definitely which college you will be attending. Then you can make sure you are taking tests your college will accept for credit. You will also be able to request that your scores be sent to the college, free of charge, when you take the tests.

If you have already taken CLEP examinations, but did not have a copy of your score report sent to your college, you may request the College Board to send an official transcript at any time for a small fee. Use the Transcript Request Form that was sent to you with your score report. If you do not have the form, you may find it online at www.collegeboard.com/clep.

Your CLEP scores will be evaluated, probably by someone in the admissions office, and sent to the registrar's office to be posted on your permanent record once you are enrolled. Procedures vary from college to college, but the process usually begins in the admissions office.

STEP 6. Ask to receive a written notice of the credit you receive for your CLEP score(s).

A written notice may save you problems later, when you submit your degree plan or file for graduation. In the event that there is a question about whether or not you earned CLEP credit, you will have an official record of what credit was awarded. You may also need this verification of course credit if you go for academic counseling before the credit is posted on your permanent record.

STEP 7. Before you register for courses, seek academic counseling.

A discussion with your academic advisor can prevent you from taking unnecessary courses and can tell you specifically what your CLEP credit will mean to you. This step may be accomplished at the time you enroll. Most colleges have orientation sessions for new students prior to each enrollment period. During orientation, students are usually assigned an academic advisor who then gives them individual help in developing long-range plans and a course schedule for the next semester. In conjunction with this counseling, you may be asked to take some additional tests so that you can be placed at the proper course level.

External Degree Programs

If you have acquired a considerable amount of college-level knowledge through job experience, reading, or noncredit courses, if you have accumulated college credits at a variety of colleges over a period of years, or if you prefer studying on your own rather than in a classroom setting, you may want to investigate the possibility of enrolling in an external degree program. Many colleges offer external degree programs that allow you to earn a degree by passing examinations (including CLEP), transferring credit from other colleges, and demonstrating in other ways that you have satisfied the educational requirements. No classroom attendance is required, and the programs are open to out-of-state candidates as well as residents. Thomas A. Edison State College in New Jersey and Charter Oaks College in Connecticut are fully accredited independent state colleges; the New York program is part of the state university system and is also fully accredited. If you are interested in exploring an external degree, you can write for more information to:

    Charter Oak College
    The Exchange, Suite 171
    270 Farmington Avenue
    Farmington, CT 06032-1909

    Regents External Degree Program
    Cultural Education Center
    Empire State Plaza
    Albany, New York 12230

    Thomas A. Edison State College
    101 West State Street
    Trenton, New Jersey 08608

Many other colleges also have external degree or weekend programs. While they often require that a number of courses be taken on campus, the external degree programs tend to be more flexible in transferring credit, granting credit-by-examination, and allowing independent study than other traditional programs. When applying to a college, you may wish to ask whether it has an external degree or weekend program.

Questions to Ask About a College's CLEP Policy

Before taking CLEP examinations for the purpose of earning college credit, try to find the answers to these questions:

1. Which CLEP examinations are accepted by this college?

A college may accept some CLEP examinations for credit and not others - possibly not the one you are considering. The English faculty may decide to grant college English credit based on the CLEP English Composition examination, but not on the Freshman College Composition examination. Or, the mathematics faculty may decide to grant credit based on the College Mathematics to non-mathematics majors only, requiring majors to take an examination in algebra, trigonometry, or calculus to earn credit. For these reasons, it is important that you know the specific CLEP tests for which you can receive credit.

2. Does the college require the optional free-response (essay) section as well as the objective portion of the CLEP examination you are considering?

Knowing the answer to this question ahead of time will permit you to schedule the optional essay examination when you register to take your CLEP examination.

3. Is credit granted for specific courses? If so, which ones?

You are likely to find that credit will be granted for specific courses and the course titles will be designated in the college's CLEP policy. It is not necessary, however, that credit be granted for a specific course in order for you to benefit from your CLEP credit. For instance, at many liberal arts colleges, all students must take certain types of courses; these courses may be labeled the core curriculum, general education requirements, distribution requirements, or liberal arts requirements. The requirements are often expressed in terms of credit hours. For example, all students may be required to take at least six hours of humanities, six hours of English, three hours of mathematics, six hours of natural science, and six hours of social science, with no particular courses in these disciplines specified. In these instances, CLEP credit may be given as 6 hrs. English credit or 3 hrs. Math credit without specifying for which English or mathematics courses credit has been awarded. In order to avoid possible disappointment, you should know before taking a CLEP examination what type of credit you can receive and whether you will only be exempted from a required course but receive no credit.

4. How much credit is granted for each examination you are considering, and does the college place a limit on the total amount of CLEP credit you can earn toward your degree?

Not all colleges that grant CLEP credit award the same amount for individual tests. Furthermore, some colleges place a limit on the total amount of credit you can earn through CLEP or other examinations. Other colleges may grant you exemption but no credit toward your degree. Knowing several colleges' policies concerning these issues may help you decide which college you will attend. If you think you are capable of passing a number of CLEP examinations, you may want to attend a college that will allow you to earn credit for all or most of them. For example, the state external degree programs grant credit for most CLEP examinations (and other tests as well).

5. What is the required score for earning CLEP credit for each test you are considering?

Most colleges publish the required scores or percentile ranks for earning CLEP credit in their general catalog or in a brochure. The required score may vary from test to test, so find out the required score for each test you are considering.

6. What is the college's policy regarding prior course work in the subject in which you are considering taking a CLEP test?

Some colleges will not grant credit for a CLEP test if the student has already attempted a college-level course closely aligned with that test. For example, if you successfully completed English 101 or a comparable course on another campus, you will probably not be permitted to receive CLEP credit in that subject, too. Some colleges will not permit you to earn CLEP credit for a course that you failed.

7. Does the college make additional stipulations before credit will be granted?

It is common practice for colleges to award CLEP credit only to their enrolled students. There are other stipulations, however, that vary from college to college. For example, does the college require you to formally apply for or accept CLEP credit by completing and signing a form? Or does the college require you to validate your CLEP score by successfully completing a more advanced course in the subject? Answers to these and other questions will help to smooth the process of earning college credit through CLEP.

The above questions and the discussions that follow them indicate some of the ways in which colleges' CLEP policies can vary. Find out as much as possible about the CLEP policies at the colleges you are interested in so you can choose a college with a policy that is compatible with your educational goals. Once you have selected the college you will attend, you can find out which CLEP examinations your college recognizes and the requirements for earning CLEP credit.

DECIDING WHICH EXAMINATIONS TO TAKE

If You're Taking the Examinations for College Credit or Career Advancement:

Most people who take CLEP examinations do so in order to earn credit for college courses. Others take the examinations in order to qualify for job promotions or for professional certification or licensing. It is vital to most candidates who are taking the tests for any of these reasons that they be well prepared for the tests they are taking so that they can advance as rapidly as possible toward their educational or career goals.

It is usually advisable that those who have limited knowledge in the subjects covered by the tests they are considering enroll in the college courses in which that material is taught. Those who are uncertain about whether or not they know enough about a subject to do well on a particular CLEP test will find the following guidelines helpful.

There is no way to predict if you will pass a particular CLEP examination, but answers to the questions under the seven headings below should give you an indication of whether or not you are likely to succeed.

1. Test Descriptions

Read the description of the test provided. Are you familiar with most of the topics and terminology in the outline?

2. Textbooks

Examine the suggested textbooks and other resource materials following the test descriptions in this guide. Have you recently read one or more of these books, or have you read similar college-level books on this subject? If you have not, read through one or more of the textbooks listed, or through the textbook used for this course at your college. Are you familiar with most of the topics and terminology in the book?

3. Sample Questions

The sample questions provided are intended to be typical of the content and difficulty of the questions on the test. Although they are not an exact miniature of the test, the proportion of the sample questions you can answer correctly should be a rough estimate of the proportion of questions you will be able to answer correctly on the test.

Answer as many of the sample questions for this test as you can. Check your answers against the correct answers. Did you answer more than half the questions correctly?

Because of variations in course content at different institutions, and because questions on CLEP tests vary from easy to difficult - with most being of moderate difficulty - the average student who passes a course in a subject can usually answer correctly about half the questions on the corresponding CLEP examination. Most colleges set their passing scores near this level, but some set them higher. If your college has set its required score above the level required by most colleges, you may need to answer a larger proportion of questions on the test correctly.

4. Previous Study

Have you taken noncredit courses in this subject offered by an adult school or a private school, through correspondence, or in connection with your job? Did you do exceptionally well in this subject in high school, or did you take an honors course in this subject?

5. Experience

Have you learned or used the knowledge or skills included in this test in your job or life experience? For example, if you lived in a Spanish-speaking country and spoke the language for a year or more, you might consider taking the Spanish examination. Or, if you have worked at a job in which you used accounting and finance skills, Principles of Accounting would be a likely test for you to take. Or, if you have read a considerable amount of literature and attended many art exhibits, concerts, and plays, you might expect to do well on the Humanities exam.

6. Other Examinations

Have you done well on other standardized tests in subjects related to the one you want to take? For example, did you score well above average on a portion of a college entrance examination covering similar skills, or did you obtain an exceptionally high score on a high school equivalency test or a licensing examination in this subject? Although such tests do not cover exactly the same material as the CLEP examinations and may be easier, persons who do well on these tests often do well on CLEP examinations, too.

7. Advice

Has a college counselor, professor, or some other professional person familiar with your ability advised you to take a CLEP examination?

If your answer was yes to questions under several of the above headings, you probably have a good chance of passing the CLEP examination you are considering. It is unlikely that you would have acquired sufficient background from experience alone. Learning gained through reading and study is essential, and you will probably find some additional study helpful before taking a CLEP examination.

If You're Taking the Examinations to Prepare for College

Many people entering college, particularly adults returning to college after several years away from formal education, are uncertain about their ability to compete with other college students. They wonder whether they have sufficient background for college study, and those who have been away from formal study for some time wonder whether they have forgotten how to study, how to take tests, and how to write papers. Such people may wish to improve their test-taking and study skills prior to enrolling in courses.

One way to assess your ability to perform at the college level and to improve your test-taking and study skills at the same time is to prepare for and take one or more CLEP examinations. You need not be enrolled in a college to take a CLEP examination, and you may have your scores sent only to yourself and later request that a transcript be sent to a college if you then decide to apply for credit. By reviewing the test descriptions and sample questions, you may find one or several subject areas in which you think you have substantial knowledge. Select one examination, or more if you like, and carefully read at least one of the textbooks listed in the bibliography for the test. By doing this, you will get a better idea of how much you know of what is usually taught in a college-level course in that subject. Study as much material as you can, until you think you have a good grasp of the subject matter. Then take the test at a college in your area. It will be several weeks before you receive your results, and you may wish to begin reviewing for another test in the meantime.

To find out if you are eligible for credit for your CLEP score, you must compare your score with the score required by the college you plan to attend. If you are not yet sure which college you will attend, or whether you will enroll in college at all, you should begin to follow the steps outlined. It is best that you do this before taking a CLEP test, but if you are taking the test only for the experience and to familiarize yourself with college-level material and requirements, you might take the test before you approach a college. Even if the college you decide to attend does not accept the test you took, the experience of taking such a test will enable you to meet with greater confidence the requirements of courses you will take.

You will find information about how to interpret your scores in WHAT YOUR SCORES MEAN, which you will receive with your score report, and which can also be found online at the CLEP website. Many colleges follow the recommendations of the American Council on Education (ACE) for setting their required scores, so you can use this information as a guide in determining how well you did. The ACE recommendations are included in the booklet.

If you do not do well enough on the test to earn college credit, don't be discouraged. Usually, it is the best college students who are exempted from courses or receive credit-by-examination. The fact that you cannot get credit for your score means that you should probably enroll in a college course to learn the material. However, if your score was close to the required score, or if you feel you could do better on a second try or after some additional study, you may retake the test after six months. Do not take it sooner or your score will not be reported and your fee will be forfeited.

If you do earn the score required to earn credit, you will have demonstrated that you already have some college-level knowledge. You will also have a better idea whether you should take additional CLEP examinations. And, what is most important, you can enroll in college with confidence, knowing that you do have the ability to succeed.

PREPARING TO TAKE CLEP EXAMINATIONS

Having made the decision to take one or more CLEP examinations, most people then want to know if it is worthwhile to prepare for them - how much, how long, when, and how should they go about it? The precise answers to these questions vary greatly from individual to individual. However, most candidates find that some type of test preparation is helpful.

Most people who take CLEP examinations do so to show that they have already learned the important material that is taught in a college course. Many of them need only a quick review to assure themselves that they have not forgotten some of what they once studied, and to fill in some of the gaps in their knowledge of the subject. Others feel that they need a thorough review and spend several weeks studying for a test. A few wish to take a CLEP examination as a kind of final examination for independent study of a subject instead of the college course. This last group requires significantly more study than those who only need to review, and they may need some guidance from professors of the subjects they are studying.

The key to how you prepare for CLEP examinations often lies in locating those skills and areas of prior learning in which you are strong and deciding where to focus your energies. Some people may know a great deal about a certain subject area, but may not test well. These individuals would probably be just as concerned about strengthening their test-taking skills as they are about studying for a specific test. Many mental and physical skills are used in preparing for a test. It is important not only to review or study for the examinations, but to make certain that you are alert, relatively free of anxiety, and aware of how to approach standardized tests. Suggestions on developing test-taking skills and preparing psychologically and physically for a test are given. The following section suggests ways of assessing your knowledge of the content of a test and then reviewing and studying the material.

Using This Study Guide

Begin by carefully reading the test description and outline of knowledge and skills required for the examination, if given. As you read through the topics listed there, ask yourself how much you know about each one. Also note the terms, names, and symbols that are mentioned, and ask yourself whether you are familiar with them. This will give you a quick overview of how much you know about the subject. If you are familiar with nearly all the material, you will probably need a minimum of review; however, if less than half of it is familiar, you will probably require substantial study to do well on the test.

If, after reviewing the test description, you find that you need extensive review, delay answering the sample question until you have done some reading in the subject. If you complete them before reviewing the material, you will probably look for the answers as you study, and then they will not be a good assessment of your ability at a later date.

If you think you are familiar with most of the test material, try to answer the sample questions.

Apply the test-taking strategies given. Keeping within the time limit suggested will give you a rough idea of how quickly you should work in order to complete the actual test.

Check your answers against the answer key. If you answered nearly all the questions correctly, you probably do not need to study the subject extensively. If you got about half the questions correct, you ought o review at least one textbook or other suggested materials on the subject. If you answered less than half the questions correctly, you will probably benefit from more extensive reading in the subject and thorough study of one or more textbooks. The textbooks listed are used at many colleges but they are not the only good texts. You will find helpful almost any standard text available to you., such as the textbook used at your college, or earlier editions of texts listed. For some examinations, topic outlines and textbooks may not be available. Take the sample tests in this book and check your answers at the end of each test. Check wrong answers.

Suggestions for Studying

The following suggestions have been gathered from people who have prepared for CLEP examinations or other college-level tests.

1. Define your goals and locate study materials

First, determine your study goals. Set aside a block of time to review the material provided in this book, and then decide which test(s) you will take. Using the suggestions, locate suitable resource materials. If a preparation course is offered by an adult school or college in your area, you might find it helpful to enroll.

2. Find a good place to study

To determine what kind of place you need for studying, ask yourself questions such as: Do I need a quiet place? Does the telephone distract me? Do objects I see in this place remind me of things I should do? Is it too warm? Is it well lit? Am I too comfortable here? Do I have space to spread out my materials? You may find the library more conducive to studying than your home. If you decide to study at home, you might prevent interruptions by other household members by putting a sign on the door of your study room to indicate when you will be available.

3. Schedule time to study

To help you determine where studying best fits into your schedule, try this exercise: Make a list of your daily activities (for example, sleeping, working, and eating) and estimate how many hours per day you spend on each activity. Now, rate all the activities on your list in order of their importance and evaluate your use of time. Often people are astonished at how an average day appears from this perspective. They may discover that they were unaware how large portions of time are spent, or they learn their time can be scheduled in alternative ways. For example, they can remove the least important activities from their day and devote that time to studying or another important activity.

4. Establish a study routine and a set of goals

In order to study effectively, you should establish specific goals and a schedule for accomplishing them. Some people find it helpful to write out a weekly schedule and cross out each study period when it is completed. Others maintain their concentration better by writing down the time when they expect to complete a study task. Most people find short periods of intense study more productive than long stretches of time. For example, they may follow a regular schedule of several 20- or 30-minute study periods with short breaks between them. Some people like to allow themselves rewards as they complete each study goal. It is not essential that you accomplish every goal exactly within your schedule; the point is to be committed to your task.

5. Learn how to take an active role in studying.

If you have not done much studying for some time, you may find it difficult to concentrate at first. Try a method of studying, such as the one outlined below, that will help you concentrate on and remember what you read.

    a. First, read the chapter summary and the introduction. Then you will know what to look for in your reading.

    b. Next, convert the section or paragraph headlines into questions. For example, if you are reading a section entitled, The Causes of the American Revolution, ask yourself: *What were the causes of the American Revolution?* Compose the answer as you read the paragraph. Reading and answering questions aloud will help you understand and remember the material.

c. Take notes on key ideas or concepts as you read. Writing will also help you fix concepts more firmly in your mind. Underlining key ideas or writing notes in your book can be helpful and will be useful for review. Underline only important points. If you underline more than a third of each paragraph, you are probably underlining too much.

   d. If there are questions or problems at the end of a chapter, answer or solve them on paper as if you were asked to do them for homework. Mathematics textbooks (and some other books) sometimes include answers to some or all of the exercises. If you have such a book, write your answers before looking at the ones given. When problem-solving is involved, work enough problems to master the required methods and concepts. If you have difficulty with problems, review any sample problems or explanations in the chapter.

   e. To retain knowledge, most people have to review the material periodically. If you are preparing for a test over an extended period of time, review key concepts and notes each week or so. Do not wait for weeks to review the material or you will need to relearn much of it.

Psychological and Physical Preparation

Most people feel at least some nervousness before taking a test. Adults who are returning to college may not have taken a test in many years or they may have had little experience with standardized tests. Some younger students, as well, are uncomfortable with testing situations. People who received their education in countries outside the United States may find that many tests given in this country are quite different from the ones they are accustomed to taking.

Not only might candidates find the types of tests and the kinds of questions on them unfamiliar, but other aspects of the testing environment may be strange as well. The physical and mental stress that results from meeting this new experience can hinder a candidate's ability to demonstrate his or her true degree of knowledge in the subject area being tested. For this reason, it is important to go to the test center well prepared, both mentally and physically, for taking the test. You may find the following suggestions helpful.

1. Familiarize yourself, as much as possible, with the test and the test situation before the day of the examination. It will be helpful for you to know ahead of time:

   a. How much time will be allowed for the test and whether there are timed subsections.

   b. What types of questions and directions appear on the examination.

   c. How your test score will be computed.

   d. How to properly answer the questions on the computer (See the CLEP Sample on the CLEP website)

e. In which building and room the examination will be administered. If you don't know where the building is, locate it or get directions ahead of time.

f. The time of the test administration. You might wish to confirm this information a day or two before the examination and find out what time the building and room will be open so that you can plan to arrive early.

g. Where to park your car or, if you wish to take public transportation, which bus or train to take and the location of the nearest stop.

h. Whether smoking will be permitted during the test.

i. Whether there will be a break between examinations (if you will be taking more than one on the same day), and whether there is a place nearby where you can get something to eat or drink.

2. Go to the test situation relaxed and alert. In order to prepare for the test:

a. Get a good night's sleep. Last minute cramming, particularly late the night before, is usually counterproductive.

b. Eat normally. It is usually not wise to skip breakfast or lunch on the day of the test or to eat a big meal just before the test.

c. Avoid tranquilizers and stimulants. If you follow the other directions in this book, you won't need artificial aids. It's better to be a little tense than to be drowsy, but stimulants such as coffee and cola can make you nervous and interfere with your concentration.

d. Don't drink a lot of liquids before the test. Having to leave the room during the test will disturb your concentration and take valuable time away from the test.

e. If you are inclined to be nervous or tense, learn some relaxation exercises and use them before and perhaps during the test.

3. Arrive for the test early and prepared. Be sure to:

a. Arrive early enough so that you can find a parking place, locate the test center, and get settled comfortably before testing begins. Allow some extra time in case you are delayed unexpectedly.

b. Take the following with you:

- Your completed Registration/Admission Form
- Two forms of identification – one being a government-issued photo ID with signature, such as a driver's license or passport
- Non-mechanical pencil
- A watch so that you can time your progress (digital watches are prohibited)
- Your glasses if you need them for reading or seeing the chalkboard or wall clock

  c. Leave all books, papers, and notes outside the test center. You will not be permitted to use your own scratch paper; it will be provided. Also prohibited are calculators, cell phones, beepers, pagers, photo/copy devices, radios, headphones, food, beverages, and several other items.

  d. Be prepared for any temperature in the testing room. Wear layers of clothing that can be removed if the room is too hot but will keep you warm if it is too cold.

4. When you enter the test room:

  a. Sit in a seat that provides a maximum of comfort and freedom from distraction.

  b. Read directions carefully, and listen to all instructions given by the test administrator. If you don't understand the directions, ask for help before test timing begins. If you must ask a question after the test has begun, raise your hand and a proctor will assist you. The proctor can answer certain kinds of questions but cannot help you with the test.

  c. Know your rights as a test taker. You can expect to be given the full working time allowed for the test(s) and a reasonably quiet and comfortable place in which to work. If a poor test situation is preventing you from doing your best, ask if the situation can be remedied. If bad test conditions cannot be remedied, ask the person in charge to report the problem in the Irregularity Report that will be sent to ETS with the answer sheets. You may also wish to contact CLEP. Describe the exact circumstances as completely as you can. Be sure to include the test date and name(s) of the test(s) you took. ETS will investigate the problem to make sure it does not happen again, and, if the problem is serious enough, may arrange for you to retake the test without charge.

TAKING THE EXAMINATIONS

A person may know a great deal about the subject being tested, but not do as well as he or she is capable of on the test. Knowing how to approach a test is an important part of the testing process. While a command of test-taking skills cannot substitute for knowledge of the subject matter, it can be a significant factor in successful testing.

Test-taking skills enable a person to use all available information to earn a score that truly reflects his or her ability. There are different strategies for approaching different kinds of test questions. For example, free-response questions require a very different tack than do multiple-choice questions. Other factors, such as how the test will be graded, may also influence your approach to the test and your use of test time. Thus, your preparation for a test should include finding out all you can about the test so that you can use the most effective test-taking strategies.

Before taking a test, you should know approximately how many questions are on the test, how much time you will be allowed, how the test will be scored or graded, what types of questions and directions are on the test, and how you will be required to record your answers.

Taking Multiple-Choice Tests

1. Listen carefully to the instructions given by the test administrator and read carefully all directions before you begin to answer the questions.

2. Note the time that the test administrator starts timing the test. As you proceed, make sure that you are not working too slowly. You should have answered at least half the questions in a section when half the time for that section has passed. If you have not reached that point in the section, speed up your pace on the remaining questions.

3. Before answering a question, read the entire question, including all the answer choices. Don't think that because the first or second answer choice looks good to you, it isn't necessary to read the remaining options. Instructions usually tell you to select the best answer. Sometimes one answer choice is partially correct, but another option is better; therefore, it is usually a good idea to read all the answers before you choose one.

4. Read and consider every question. Questions that look complicated at first glance may not actually be so difficult once you have read them carefully.

5. Do not puzzle too long over any one question. If you don't know the answer after you've considered it briefly, go on to the next question. Make sure you return to the question later.

6. Make sure you record your response properly.

7. In trying to determine the correct answer, you may find it helpful to cross out those options that you know are incorrect, and to make marks next to those you think might be correct. If you decide to skip the question and come back to it later, you will save yourself the time of reconsidering all the options.

8. Watch for the following key words in test questions:

all	generally	never	perhaps
always	however	none	rarely
but	may	not	seldom
except	must	often	sometimes
every	necessary	only	usually

When a question or answer option contains words such as always, every, only, never, and none, there can be no exceptions to the answer you choose. Use of words such as often, rarely, sometimes, and generally indicates that there may be some exceptions to the answer.

9. Do not waste your time looking for clues to right answers based on flaws in question wording or patterns in correct answers. Professionals at the College Board and ETS put

a great deal of effort into developing valid, reliable, fair tests. CLEP test development committees are composed of college faculty who are experts in the subject covered by the test and are appointed by the College Board to write test questions and to scrutinize each question that is included on a CLEP test. Committee members make every effort to ensure that the questions are not ambiguous, that they have only one correct answer, and that they cover college-level topics. These committees do not intentionally include trick questions. If you think a question is flawed, ask the test administrator to report it, or contact CLEP immediately.

Taking Free-Response or Essay Tests

If your college requires the optional free-response or essay portion of a CLEP Composition and Literature exams, you should do some additional preparation for your CLEP test. Taking an essay test is very different from taking a multiple-choice test, so you will need to use some other strategies.

The essay written as part of the English Composition and Essay exam is graded by English professors from a variety of colleges and universities. A process called holistic scoring is used to rate your writing ability.

The optional free-response essays, on the other hand, are graded by the faculty of the college you designate as a score recipient. Guidelines and criteria for grading essays are not specified by the College Board or ETS. You may find it helpful, therefore, to talk with someone at your college to find out what criteria will be used to determine whether you will get credit. If the test requires essay responses, ask how much emphasis will be placed on your writing ability and your ability to organize your thoughts as opposed to your knowledge of subject matter. Find out how much weight will be given to your multiple-choice test score in comparison with your free-response grade in determining whether you will get credit. This will give you an idea where you should expend the greatest effort in preparing for and taking the test.

Here are some strategies you will find useful in taking any essay test:

1. Before you begin to write, read all questions carefully and take a few minutes to jot down some ideas you might include in each answer.

2. If you are given a choice of questions to answer, choose the questions you think you can answer most clearly and knowledgeably.

3. Determine in what order you will answer the questions. Answer those you find the easiest first so that any extra time can be spent on the more difficult questions.

4. When you know which questions you will answer and in what order, determine how much testing time remains and estimate how many minutes you will devote to each question. Unless suggested times are given for the questions or one question appears to require more or less time than the others, allot an equal amount of time to each question.

5. Before answering each question, indicate the number of the question as it is given in the test book. You need not copy the entire question from the question sheet, but it will be helpful to you and to the person grading your test if you indicate briefly the topic you are addressing – particularly if you are not answering the questions in the order in which they appear on the test.

6. Before answering each question, read it again carefully to make sure you are interpreting it correctly. Underline key words, such as those listed below, that often appear in free-response questions. Be sure you know the exact meaning of these words before taking the test.

analyze	demonstrate	enumerate	list
apply	derive	explain	outline
assess	describe	generalize	prove
compare	determine	illustrate	rank
contrast	discuss	interpret	show
define	distinguish	justify	summarize

If a question asks you to outline, define, or summarize, do not write a detailed explanation; if a question asks you to analyze, explain, illustrate, interpret, or show, you must do more than briefly describe the topic.

For a current listing of CLEP Colleges

where you can get credit and be tested, write:

CLEP, P.O. Box 6600, Princeton, NJ 08541-6600

Or e-mail: clep@ets.org, or call: (609) 771-7865

Principles of Microeconomics

Description of the Examination

The Principles of Microeconomics examination covers material that is usually taught in a one-semester undergraduate course in introductory microeconomics. This aspect of economics deals with the principles of economics that apply to the analysis of the behavior of individual consumers and businesses in the economy. Questions on this exam require candidates to apply analytical techniques to hypothetical as well as real-world situations and to analyze and evaluate economic decisions. Candidates are expected to demonstrate an understanding of how free markets work and allocate resources efficiently. They should understand how individual consumers make economic decisions to maximize utility, and how individual firms make decisions to maximize profits. Candidates must be able to identify the characteristics of the different market structures and analyze the behavior of firms in terms of price and output decisions. They should also be able to evaluate the outcome in each market structure with respect to economic efficiency, identify cases in which private markets fail to allocate resources efficiently, and explain how government intervention fixes or fails to fix the resource allocation problem. It is also important to understand the determination of wages and other input prices in factor markets, and analyze and evaluate the distribution of income.

The examination contains approximately 80 questions to be answered in 90 minutes. Some of these are pretest questions that will not be scored. Any time candidates spend on tutorials and providing personal information is in addition to the actual testing time.

Knowledge and Skills Required

Questions on the Principles of Microeconomics examination require candidates to demonstrate one or more of the following abilities:

Understanding of important economic terms and concepts
Interpretation and manipulation of economic graphs
Interpretation and evaluation of economic data
Application of simple economic models

The subject matter of the Principles of Microeconomics examination is drawn from the following topics. The percentages next to the main topics indicate the approximate percentage of exam questions on that topic.

8-14% Basic Economic Concepts

- Scarcity, choice, and opportunity cost
- Production possibilities curve
- Comparative advantage, specialization, and trade
- Economic systems
- Property rights and the role of incentives
- Marginal analysis

From the official announcement for instructional purposes

10-18% Factor Markets

Derived factor demand
Marginal revenue product
Labor market and firms' hiring of labor
Market distribution of income

12-18% Market Failure and the Role of Government

Externalities
- Marginal social benefit and marginal social cost
- Positive externalities
- Negative externalities
- Remedies

Public goods
- Public versus private goods
- Provision of public goods

Public policy to promote competition
- Antitrust policy
- Regulation

Income distribution
- Equity
- Sources of income inequality

ECONOMISTS

NATURE OF THE WORK

Economists study the ways a society uses scarce resources such as land, labor, raw materials, and machinery to produce goods and services. They analyze the costs and benefits of distributing and consuming these goods and services. Their research might focus on topics such as energy costs, electronic components production, farm prices, or imports.

Some economists who are primarily theoreticians may develop theories through the use of mathematical models to explain the causes of business cycles and inflation or the effects of unemployment and tax policy. Most economists, however, are concerned with practical applications of economic policy in a particular area, such as finance, labor, agriculture, transportation, energy, or health. They use their understanding of economic relationships to advise business firms, insurance companies, banks, securities firms, industry associations, labor unions, government agencies, and others.

Depending on the topic under study, economists devise methods and procedures for obtaining data they need. For example, sampling techniques may be used to conduct a survey, and econometric modeling techniques may be used to develop projections. Preparing reports usually is an important part of the economist's job. He or she may be called upon to review and analyze all the relevant data, prepare tables and charts, and write up the results in clear, concise language.

Being able to present economic and statistical concepts in a meaningful way is particularly important for economists whose research is policy directed. Market research analysts who work for business firms may be asked to provide management with information to make decisions on marketing and pricing of company products; to look at the advisability of adding new lines of merchandise, opening new branches, or diversifying the company's operations; to analyze the effect of changes in the tax, laws; or to prepare economic and business forecasts. Business economists working for firms that carry on operations abroad may be asked to prepare forecasts of foreign economic conditions.

Economists who work for government agencies assess economic conditions in the United States and abroad and estimate the economic impact of specific changes in legislation or public policy. For example, they may study how changes in the minimum wage affect teenage unemployment. Most government economists are in the fields of agriculture, business, finance, labor, transportation, utilities, urban economics, or international trade. For example, economists in the U.S. Department of Commerce study domestic production, distribution, and consumption of commodities or services; those in the Federal Trade Commission prepare industry analyses to assist in enforcing Federal statutes designed to eliminate unfair, deceptive, or monopolistic practices in interstate commerce; and those in the Bureau of Labor Statistics analyze data on prices, wages, employment, and productivity.

WORKING CONDITIONS

Economists working for government agencies and private firms have structured work schedules. They may work alone writing reports, preparing statistical charts, and using computers and calculators. Or they may be an integral part of a research team. Most work under pressure of deadlines and tight schedules, and sometimes must work overtime. Their routine may be interrupted by special requests for data, letters, meetings, or conferences. Travel may be necessary to collect data or attend conferences.

Economics faculty has flexible work schedules, dividing their time among teaching, research, consulting, and administrative responsibilities.

EMPLOYMENT

Economists hold about 15,000 jobs. Private industry -- particularly economic and market research firms, management consulting firms, advertising firms, banks, and securities, investment, and insurance companies -- employed over two-thirds of all salaried economists. The remainders were employed by a wide range of government agencies, primarily in the Federal Government. The Department of Labor, Agriculture, and State are the largest Federal employers. About one out of every five economists runs his or her own consulting business. A number of economists combine a full-time job in government or business with part-time or -consulting work in another setting.

Employment of economists is concentrated in large cities. The largest numbers are in New York City and Washington, D.C. Some work abroad for companies with major international operations; for the Department of State and other U.S. Government agencies; and for international organizations.

Besides the jobs described above, an estimated 30,000 persons held economics and marketing faculty positions in colleges and universities.

TRAINING, OTHER QUALIFICATIONS, AND ADVANCEMENT

A bachelor's degree with a major in economics or marketing is sufficient for many beginning research, administrative, management trainee, and sales jobs. The undergraduate curriculum includes courses such as microeconomics, macroeconomics, business cycles, economic and business history, and economic development of selected areas, money and banking, international economics, public finance, industrial organization, labor economics, comparative economic systems, economics of national planning, urban economic problems, marketing, and consumer behavior analysis. Courses in related disciplines, such as political science, psychology, organizational behavior, sociology, finance, business law, and international relations, are suggested. Because of the importance of quantitative skills to economists, courses in mathematics, business and economic statistics, sampling theory and survey design, and computer science are highly recommended.

Graduate training increasingly is required for most economist jobs and for advancement to more responsible positions. Areas of specialization at the graduate level include advanced economic theory, mathematical economics, econometrics, history of economic thought, and comparative economic systems and planning. Other areas include economic history, economic development, environmental and natural resource economics, industrial organization, marketing, institutional economics, international economics, labor economics, monetary economics, public finance, regional and urban economics, and social policy. Students should select graduate schools strong in specialties in which they are interested. Some schools help graduate students find internships or part-time employment in government agencies, economic consulting firms, financial institutions, or market research firms. Work experience and contacts can be useful in testing career preference and learning about the job market for economists.

In the Federal Government, candidates for entrance positions generally need a college degree with a minimum of 21 semester hours of economics and 3 hours of statistics, accounting, or calculus. However, because competition is keen, additional education or experience may be required.

For a job as a college instructor in many junior colleges and small 4-year schools, a master's degree generally is the minimum requirement. In some colleges and universities, however, a Ph.D. and extensive publication are required for a professorship and for tenure, which are increasingly difficult to obtain.

In government, industry, research organizations, and consulting firms, economists who have a graduate degree usually can qualify for more responsible research and administrative positions. A Ph.D. is necessary for top positions in many organizations. Many corporation and government executives have a strong background in economics or marketing.

Over 1,200 colleges and universities offer bachelor's degree programs in economics and marketing; over 600, masters and about 130, doctoral programs.

Persons considering careers as economists should be able to work accurately with detail since much time is spent on data analysis. Patience and persistence are necessary because economists may spend long hours on independent study and problem solving. At the same time, they must be able to work well with others. Economists must be objective and systematic in their work and be able to express themselves effectively both orally and in writing. Creativity and intellectual curiosity are essential for success in this field, just as they are in other areas of scientific endeavor.

JOB OUTLOOK

Employment of economists is expected to grow at a slower rate than the average for all occupations in the next decade. Most job openings, however, will result from the need to replace experienced economists who transfer to other occupations, or retire or leave the labor force for other reasons.

Opportunities should be best in manufacturing, financial services, advertising agencies, research organizations, and consulting firms, reflecting the complexity of the domestic and international economies and increased reliance on quantitative methods of analyzing business trends, forecasting sales, and planning of purchasing and production. The continued need for economic analyses by lawyers, accountants, engineers, health service administrators, urban and regional planners, environmental scientists, and others will also increase the number of jobs for economists. Little or no change is expected in the employment of economists in the Federal Government – in line with the rate of growth projected for the Federal work force as a whole. Employment of economists in State and local government combined is expected to grow more slowly than the average.

A strong background in economic theory, statistics, and econometrics provides the tools for acquiring any specialty within the field. Those skilled in quantitative techniques and their application to economic modeling and forecasting and market research, including the use of computers, should have the best job opportunities.

Persons who graduate with a bachelor's degree in economics should face very keen competition for the limited number of economist positions for which they qualify. However, many will find employment in government, industry, and business as management or sales trainees, or as research or administrative assistants. Those with strong backgrounds in mathematics, statistics, survey design, and computer science may be hired by private firms for market research work. Those who meet State certification requirements may become high school economics teachers. (For additional information, see the statement on secondary school teachers elsewhere in the Handbook.)

Candidates who hold master's degrees in economics face very strong competition, particularly for teaching positions in colleges and universities. However, some may gain positions in junior and community colleges. Those with a strong background in marketing and finance may have the best prospects in business, banking, advertising, and management consulting firms.

Ph.D.'s are likely to face competition for academic positions, although top graduates from leading universities should have little difficulty in acquiring teaching jobs. Some will have to accept jobs at smaller or lower paying institutions. Ph.D.'s should have favorable opportunities to work as economists in government, industry, educational and research organizations, and consulting firms.

RELATED OCCUPATIONS

Economists are concerned with understanding and interpreting financial matters, among other subjects. Others with jobs in this area include financial managers, financial analysts, accountants and auditors, underwriters, actuaries, securities and financial services sales workers, credit analysts" loan officers, and budget officers.

SOURCES OF ADDITIONAL INFORMATION

National Association for Business Economics,
1223 20th St. NW, Suite 505, Washington, DC 20036 (Internet: http://www.nabe.com)

HOW TO TAKE A TEST

You have studied long, hard and conscientiously.

With your official admission card in hand, and your heart pounding, you have been admitted to the examination room.

You note that there are several hundred other applicants in the examination room waiting to take the same test.

They all appear to be equally well prepared.

You know that nothing but your best effort will suffice. The "moment of truth" is at hand: you now have to demonstrate objectively, in writing, your knowledge of content and your understanding of subject matter.

You are fighting the most important battle of your life—to pass and/or score high on an examination which will determine your career and provide the economic basis for your livelihood.

What extra, special things should you know and should you do in taking the examination?

I. YOU MUST PASS AN EXAMINATION

A. WHAT EVERY CANDIDATE SHOULD KNOW
Examination applicants often ask us for help in preparing for the written test. What can I study in advance? What kinds of questions will be asked? How will the test be given? How will the papers be graded?

B. HOW ARE EXAMS DEVELOPED?
Examinations are carefully written by trained technicians who are specialists in the field known as "psychological measurement," in consultation with recognized authorities in the field of work that the test will cover. These experts recommend the subject matter areas or skills to be tested; only those knowledges or skills important to your success on the job are included. The most reliable books and source materials available are used as references. Together, the experts and technicians judge the difficulty level of the questions.
Test technicians know how to phrase questions so that the problem is clearly stated. Their ethics do not permit "trick" or "catch" questions. Questions may have been tried out on sample groups, or subjected to statistical analysis, to determine their usefulness.
Written tests are often used in combination with performance tests, ratings of training and experience, and oral interviews. All of these measures combine to form the best-known means of finding the right person for the right job.

II. HOW TO PASS THE WRITTEN TEST

A. BASIC STEPS

1) Study the announcement

How, then, can you know what subjects to study? Our best answer is: "Learn as much as possible about the class of positions for which you've applied." The exam will test the knowledge, skills and abilities needed to do the work.

Your most valuable source of information about the position you want is the official exam announcement. This announcement lists the training and experience qualifications. Check these standards and apply only if you come reasonably close to meeting them. Many jurisdictions preview the written test in the exam announcement by including a section called "Knowledge and Abilities Required," "Scope of the Examination," or some similar heading. Here you will find out specifically what fields will be tested.

2) Choose appropriate study materials

If the position for which you are applying is technical or advanced, you will read more advanced, specialized material. If you are already familiar with the basic principles of your field, elementary textbooks would waste your time. Concentrate on advanced textbooks and technical periodicals. Think through the concepts and review difficult problems in your field.

These are all general sources. You can get more ideas on your own initiative, following these leads. For example, training manuals and publications of the government agency which employs workers in your field can be useful, particularly for technical and professional positions. A letter or visit to the government department involved may result in more specific study suggestions, and certainly will provide you with a more definite idea of the exact nature of the position you are seeking.

3) Study this book!

III. KINDS OF TESTS

Tests are used for purposes other than measuring knowledge and ability to perform specified duties. For some positions, it is equally important to test ability to make adjustments to new situations or to profit from training. In others, basic mental abilities not dependent on information are essential. Questions which test these things may not appear as pertinent to the duties of the position as those which test for knowledge and information. Yet they are often highly important parts of a fair examination. For very general questions, it is almost impossible to help you direct your study efforts. What we can do is to point out some of the more common of these general abilities needed in public service positions and describe some typical questions.

1) General information

Broad, general information has been found useful for predicting job success in some kinds of work. This is tested in a variety of ways, from vocabulary lists to questions about current events. Basic background in some field of work, such as sociology or economics, may be sampled in a group of questions. Often these are principles which have become familiar to most persons through exposure rather than through formal training. It is difficult to advise you how to study for these questions; being alert to the world around you is our best suggestion.

2) Verbal ability

An example of an ability needed in many positions is verbal or language ability. Verbal ability is, in brief, the ability to use and understand words. Vocabulary and grammar tests are typical measures of this ability. Reading comprehension or paragraph interpretation questions are common in many kinds of civil service tests. You are given a paragraph of written material and asked to find its central meaning.

IV. KINDS OF QUESTIONS

1. Multiple-choice Questions

Most popular of the short-answer questions is the "multiple choice" or "best answer" question. It can be used, for example, to test for factual knowledge, ability to solve problems or judgment in meeting situations found at work.

A multiple-choice question is normally one of three types:
- It can begin with an incomplete statement followed by several possible endings. You are to find the one ending which best completes the statement, although some of the others may not be entirely wrong.
- It can also be a complete statement in the form of a question which is answered by choosing one of the statements listed.
- It can be in the form of a problem – again you select the best answer.

Here is an example of a multiple-choice question with a discussion which should give you some clues as to the method for choosing the right answer:

When an employee has a complaint about his assignment, the action which will best help him overcome his difficulty is to
    A. discuss his difficulty with his coworkers
    B. take the problem to the head of the organization
    C. take the problem to the person who gave him the assignment
    D. say nothing to anyone about his complaint

In answering this question, you should study each of the choices to find which is best. Consider choice "A" – Certainly an employee may discuss his complaint with fellow employees, but no change or improvement can result, and the complaint remains unresolved. Choice "B" is a poor choice since the head of the organization probably does not know what assignment you have been given, and taking your problem to him is known as "going over the head" of the supervisor. The supervisor, or person who made the assignment, is the person who can clarify it or correct any injustice. Choice "C" is, therefore, correct. To say nothing, as in choice "D," is unwise. Supervisors have and interest in knowing the problems employees are facing, and the employee is seeking a solution to his problem.

2. True/False

3. Matching Questions

Matching an answer from a column of choices within another column.

V. RECORDING YOUR ANSWERS

Computer terminals are used more and more today for many different kinds of exams.

For an examination with very few applicants, you may be told to record your answers in the test booklet itself. Separate answer sheets are much more common. If this separate answer sheet is to be scored by machine – and this is often the case – it is highly important that you mark your answers correctly in order to get credit.

VI. BEFORE THE TEST

YOUR PHYSICAL CONDITION IS IMPORTANT

If you are not well, you can't do your best work on tests. If you are half asleep, you can't do your best either. Here are some tips:

1) Get about the same amount of sleep you usually get. Don't stay up all night before the test, either partying or worrying—DON'T DO IT!
2) If you wear glasses, be sure to wear them when you go to take the test. This goes for hearing aids, too.
3) If you have any physical problems that may keep you from doing your best, be sure to tell the person giving the test. If you are sick or in poor health, you relay cannot do your best on any test. You can always come back and take the test some other time.

Common sense will help you find procedures to follow to get ready for an examination. Too many of us, however, overlook these sensible measures. Indeed, nervousness and fatigue have been found to be the most serious reasons why applicants fail to do their best on civil service tests. Here is a list of reminders:

- Begin your preparation early – Don't wait until the last minute to go scurrying around for books and materials or to find out what the position is all about.
- Prepare continuously – An hour a night for a week is better than an all-night cram session. This has been definitely established. What is more, a night a week for a month will return better dividends than crowding your study into a shorter period of time.
- Locate the place of the exam – You have been sent a notice telling you when and where to report for the examination. If the location is in a different town or otherwise unfamiliar to you, it would be well to inquire the best route and learn something about the building.
- Relax the night before the test – Allow your mind to rest. Do not study at all that night. Plan some mild recreation or diversion; then go to bed early and get a good night's sleep.
- Get up early enough to make a leisurely trip to the place for the test – This way unforeseen events, traffic snarls, unfamiliar buildings, etc. will not upset you.
- Dress comfortably – A written test is not a fashion show. You will be known by number and not by name, so wear something comfortable.
- Leave excess paraphernalia at home – Shopping bags and odd bundles will get in your way. You need bring only the items mentioned in the official notice you received; usually everything you need is provided. Do not bring reference books to the exam. They will only confuse those last minutes and be taken away from you when in the test room.

- Arrive somewhat ahead of time – If because of transportation schedules you must get there very early, bring a newspaper or magazine to take your mind off yourself while waiting.
- Locate the examination room – When you have found the proper room, you will be directed to the seat or part of the room where you will sit. Sometimes you are given a sheet of instructions to read while you are waiting. Do not fill out any forms until you are told to do so; just read them and be prepared.
- Relax and prepare to listen to the instructions
- If you have any physical problem that may keep you from doing your best, be sure to tell the test administrator. If you are sick or in poor health, you really cannot do your best on the exam. You can come back and take the test some other time.

VII. AT THE TEST

The day of the test is here and you have the test booklet in your hand. The temptation to get going is very strong. Caution! There is more to success than knowing the right answers. You must know how to identify your papers and understand variations in the type of short-answer question used in this particular examination. Follow these suggestions for maximum results from your efforts:

1) Cooperate with the monitor
The test administrator has a duty to create a situation in which you can be as much at ease as possible. He will give instructions, tell you when to begin, check to see that you are marking your answer sheet correctly, and so on. He is not there to guard you, although he will see that your competitors do not take unfair advantage. He wants to help you do your best.

2) Listen to all instructions
Don't jump the gun! Wait until you understand all directions. In most civil service tests you get more time than you need to answer the questions. So don't be in a hurry. Read each word of instructions until you clearly understand the meaning. Study the examples, listen to all announcements and follow directions. Ask questions if you do not understand what to do.

3) Identify your papers
Civil service exams are usually identified by number only. You will be assigned a number; you must not put your name on your test papers. Be sure to copy your number correctly. Since more than one exam may be given, copy your exact examination title.

4) Plan your time
Unless you are told that a test is a "speed" or "rate of work" test, speed itself is usually not important. Time enough to answer all the questions will be provided, but this does not mean that you have all day. An overall time limit has been set. Divide the total time (in minutes) by the number of questions to determine the approximate time you have for each question.

5) Do not linger over difficult questions
If you come across a difficult question, mark it with a paper clip (useful to have along) and come back to it when you have been through the booklet. One caution if you do this – be sure to skip a number on your answer sheet as well. Check often to be sure that

you have not lost your place and that you are marking in the row numbered the same as the question you are answering.

6) Read the questions

Be sure you know what the question asks! Many capable people are unsuccessful because they failed to read the questions correctly.

7) Answer all questions

Unless you have been instructed that a penalty will be deducted for incorrect answers, it is better to guess than to omit a question.

8) Speed tests

It is often better NOT to guess on speed tests. It has been found that on timed tests people are tempted to spend the last few seconds before time is called in marking answers at random – without even reading them – in the hope of picking up a few extra points. To discourage this practice, the instructions may warn you that your score will be "corrected" for guessing. That is, a penalty will be applied. The incorrect answers will be deducted from the correct ones, or some other penalty formula will be used.

9) Review your answers

If you finish before time is called, go back to the questions you guessed or omitted to give them further thought. Review other answers if you have time.

10) Return your test materials

If you are ready to leave before others have finished or time is called, take ALL your materials to the monitor and leave quietly. Never take any test material with you. The monitor can discover whose papers are not complete, and taking a test booklet may be grounds for disqualification.

VIII. EXAMINATION TECHNIQUES

1) Read the general instructions carefully. These are usually printed on the first page of the exam booklet. As a rule, these instructions refer to the timing of the examination; the fact that you should not start work until the signal and must stop work at a signal, etc. If there are any special instructions, such as a choice of questions to be answered, make sure that you note this instruction carefully.

2) When you are ready to start work on the examination, that is as soon as the signal has been given, read the instructions to each question booklet, underline any key words or phrases, such as least, best, outline, describe and the like. In this way you will tend to answer as requested rather than discover on reviewing your paper that you listed without describing, that you selected the worst choice rather than the best choice, etc.

3) If the examination is of the objective or multiple-choice type – that is, each question will also give a series of possible answers: A, B, C or D, and you are called upon to select the best answer and write the letter next to that answer on your answer paper – it is advisable to start answering each question in turn. There may be anywhere from 50 to 100 such questions in the three or four hours allotted and you can see how much time would be taken if you read through all the questions before beginning to answer any. Furthermore, if you

come across a question or group of questions which you know would be difficult to answer, it would undoubtedly affect your handling of all the other questions.

4) If the examination is of the essay type and contains but a few questions, it is a moot point as to whether you should read all the questions before starting to answer any one. Of course, if you are given a choice – say five out of seven and the like – then it is essential to read all the questions so you can eliminate the two that are most difficult. If, however, you are asked to answer all the questions, there may be danger in trying to answer the easiest one first because you may find that you will spend too much time on it. The best technique is to answer the first question, then proceed to the second, etc.

5) Time your answers. Before the exam begins, write down the time it started, then add the time allowed for the examination and write down the time it must be completed, then divide the time available somewhat as follows:
   - If 3-1/2 hours are allowed, that would be 210 minutes. If you have 80 objective-type questions, that would be an average of 2-1/2 minutes per question. Allow yourself no more than 2 minutes per question, or a total of 160 minutes, which will permit about 50 minutes to review.
   - If for the time allotment of 210 minutes there are 7 essay questions to answer, that would average about 30 minutes a question. Give yourself only 25 minutes per question so that you have about 35 minutes to review.

6) The most important instruction is to read each question and make sure you know what is wanted. The second most important instruction is to time yourself properly so that you answer every question. The third most important instruction is to answer every question. Guess if you have to but include something for each question. Remember that you will receive no credit for a blank and will probably receive some credit if you write something in answer to an essay question. If you guess a letter – say "B" for a multiple-choice question – you may have guessed right. If you leave a blank as an answer to a multiple-choice question, the examiners may respect your feelings but it will not add a point to your score. Some exams may penalize you for wrong answers, so in such cases only, you may not want to guess unless you have some basis for your answer.

7) Suggestions
   a. Objective-type questions
      1. Examine the question booklet for proper sequence of pages and questions
      2. Read all instructions carefully
      3. Skip any question which seems too difficult; return to it after all other questions have been answered
      4. Apportion your time properly; do not spend too much time on any single question or group of questions
      5. Note and underline key words – all, most, fewest, least, best, worst, same, opposite, etc.
      6. Pay particular attention to negatives
      7. Note unusual option, e.g., unduly long, short, complex, different or similar in content to the body of the question
      8. Observe the use of "hedging" words – probably, may, most likely, etc.

9. Make sure that your answer is put next to the same number as the question
10. Do not second-guess unless you have good reason to believe the second answer is definitely more correct
11. Cross out original answer if you decide another answer is more accurate; do not erase until you are ready to hand your paper in
12. Answer all questions; guess unless instructed otherwise
13. Leave time for review

b. Essay questions
   1. Read each question carefully
   2. Determine exactly what is wanted. Underline key words or phrases.
   3. Decide on outline or paragraph answer
   4. Include many different points and elements unless asked to develop any one or two points or elements
   5. Show impartiality by giving pros and cons unless directed to select one side only
   6. Make and write down any assumptions you find necessary to answer the questions
   7. Watch your English, grammar, punctuation and choice of words
   8. Time your answers; don't crowd material

8) Answering the essay question

Most essay questions can be answered by framing the specific response around several key words or ideas. Here are a few such key words or ideas:

M's: manpower, materials, methods, money, management
P's: purpose, program, policy, plan, procedure, practice, problems, pitfalls, personnel, public relations

a. Six basic steps in handling problems:
   1. Preliminary plan and background development
   2. Collect information, data and facts
   3. Analyze and interpret information, data and facts
   4. Analyze and develop solutions as well as make recommendations
   5. Prepare report and sell recommendations
   6. Install recommendations and follow up effectiveness

b. Pitfalls to avoid
1. Taking things for granted – A statement of the situation does not necessarily imply that each of the elements is necessarily true; for example, a complaint may be invalid and biased so that all that can be taken for granted is that a complaint has been registered
2. Considering only one side of a situation – Wherever possible, indicate several alternatives and then point out the reasons you selected the best one
3. Failing to indicate follow up – Whenever your answer indicates action on your part, make certain that you will take proper follow-up action to see how successful your recommendations, procedures or actions turn out to be
4. Taking too long in answering any single question – Remember to time your answers properly

EXAMINATION SECTION

EXAMINATION SECTION
TEST 1

DIRECTIONS: Each question or incomplete statement is followed by several suggested answers or completions. Select the one that BEST answers the question or completes the statement. *PRINT THE LETTER OF THE CORRECT ANSWER IN THE SPACE AT THE RIGHT.*

1. What is the fundamental concept on which all economics rests?

    A. Scarcity
    B. Production
    C. Capital
    D. Consumption
    E. Profits and losses

2. Which of the following are TRUE of corporations?
    I. Only bondholders and preferred stockholders have voting rights.
    II. Only bondholders are considered creditors.
    III. Common stockholders only receive dividends after the preferred stockholders have been paid.
    IV. Only preferred stockholders elect the board of directors.
    V. Preferred stockholders must receive dividends if there are profits.

    The CORRECT answer is:

    A. I, IV, V
    B. II, III
    C. II, IV
    D. II, III, IV, V
    E. All of the above

3. Which of the following are TRUE of marginal revenue of the competitive firm in a perfect market?
    I. Additional revenue is dependent on the prevailing market price.
    II. The expansion of individual firms affects price within the market.
    III. The demand curve faced by the producer of commodities is infinitely elastic.
    IV. The marginal revenue curve is the demand curve.
    V. Marginal revenue occurs when the individual firm sells below the prevailing market price.

    The CORRECT answer is:

    A. I, III, IV
    B. I, II
    C. I, III, V
    D. II, III, V
    E. II, V

4. Malthusian economics has not proved accurate MAINLY because

    A. the population has not expanded geometrically
    B. of technological advances
    C. land resources are still relatively abundant
    D. of a shift in the demand curve
    E. of the productivity of the labor force

5. What is the MAIN difference between monopolistic competition and pure competition? The

    A. products offered for sale
    B. number of sellers

1

C. ease of entry into the industry
D. ease of exit from the industry
E. control over price

6. Oligopolies producing a heterogeneous product compete by

   A. cutting prices
   B. improving their product
   C. duplicating price changes of the industry leader
   D. regulating production
   E. cutting production costs

7. Which of the main problems that are the subject matter of microeconomics is the LEAST controversial?
   The

   A. potential of the economy to produce
   B. rate of growth of production
   C. type and quantity of a commodity to be produced
   D. distribution of goods and services
   E. size of the market

8. Why does the hourly rate have to increase? To

   A. prevent strikes
   B. ensure maximum production
   C. inspire technological advances
   D. increase the number of man-hours supplied per annum
   E. maintain the standard of living of American workers

9. Which of the following probably have an inelastic demand curve?
   A commodity
   I. that represents a fraction of the consumer's income
   II. that has good substitutes available in the market
   III. of a particular industry as a whole
   IV. that is highly durable
   V. that is easily maintained
   The CORRECT answer is:

   A. I, III, IV   B. II, IV
   C. I, III   D. II, V
   E. II, III, IV, V

10. The state of technology of the firm is summarized by the

    A. level of production   B. simplex method
    C. entrepreneur   D. process of production
    E. production function

11. The perfect market may be described as

    A. a planned economy   B. monopolistic competition
    C. heterogeneous   D. monopolistic
    E. purely competitive

12. All of the following are true of the price-support program EXCEPT: 12.____

    A. Efficient farmers reap a risk-free bumper money crop year after year
    B. The price support program is sufficiently high to cover variable costs, the cost of capital, and land rents
    C. The price-support program leaves farm operators with an income higher than their opportunity income in the non-farm sector
    D. It weakens the incentive of marginal farmers to migrate
    E. The government is left with enormous surpluses

13. The exploitation of consumers is measured by 13.____

    A. market elasticity
    B. comparing marginal revenue with marginal cost
    C. the difference between price and fixed cost
    D. the difference between price and marginal cost
    E. the difference between price and marginal revenue

14. Profits occur as a consequence of all of the following reasons EXCEPT 14.____

    A. risk taking
    B. a limited supply of specific resources
    C. contrived scarcities
    D. monopolistic power over markets
    E. production matching demand

15. The MAIN reason for a rate of interest is to 15.____

    A. reward savers for abstaining from consumption
    B. induce firms to invest
    C. encourage future consumption
    D. provide for a more equal distribution of income
    E. encourage the flow of money through the market

16. Demand is relatively inelastic when 16.____

    A. the percentage change in the quantity demanded is smaller than the percentage change in the price
    B. the percentage change in the quantity demanded is larger than the percentage change in the price
    C. the percentage change in the quantity demanded is equal to the percentage change in the price
    D. a one-percent change in price will induce more than a one-percent change in the quantity demanded
    E. a one-percent change in the price will induce less than a one-percent change in the quantity demanded

17. How does a corporation differ from either a single proprietorship or a partnership? 17.____

    A. It has the advantage of flexibility.
    B. It has a limited capacity to raise capital.
    C. The liability of the owner is limited.
    D. It has a better credit standing.
    E. It is most useful for firms that require relatively little capital.

18. In a perfect market, a firm maximizes its profits when it   18.____

    A. expands to maximum potential of production
    B. expands and contracts in response to the prevailing price
    C. operates at that point where the marginal cost equals the price
    D. operates at the point where the prevailing price is at its apex
    E. expands to the point where the marginal revenue exceeds the market place

19. All of the following are elements of a planned economy EXCEPT: 19.____

    A. Price mechanism is very much limited
    B. Existence of a black market
    C. Producers expand or contract along the supply curve
    D. Shortages are difficult to detect
    E. Production quotas are not related to profits

20. All of the following are TRUE of oligopoly EXCEPT   20.____

    A. few sellers
    B. no close substitutes for the product or service
    C. greater likelihood for collusion in setting prices
    D. primarily non-price competition
    E. some difficulty of entry into the industry

21. Which of the following is NOT a reason why oligopolies producing a differentiated prod-   21.____
    uct adhere to a policy of sluggish prices?
    Because

    A. of tradition
    B. of tacit agreement
    C. the administrative cost of changing prices is too high
    D. of fear of a price war
    E. of government regulation

22. What determines the well-being of the various classes of society?   22.____
    The

    A. process of distribution   B. process of setting prices
    C. factors of production   D. markets for resources
    E. monetary flow

23. The utility of future consumption is smaller than the utility of present consumption   23.____
    because of

    A. profits   B. elasticity
    C. interest rates   D. the supply curve
    E. uncertainty

24. Which of the following sequences identifies the mobility of resource supplies in the short   24.____
    run from least to most mobile?

    A. Labor, land, capital   B. Land, labor, capital
    C. Labor, capital, land   D. Land, capital, labor
    E. Capital, land, labor

25. The size of the perfect market place depends on the
    I. number of consumers
    II. homogeneity of the commodity
    III. relative cost of shipping
    IV. extent of competition
    V. cost of obtaining information about the market
    The CORRECT answer is:

    A. I, III, IV
    B. I, II, III
    C. I, IV
    D. II, III, V
    E. All of the above

26. Which of the following are examples of businesses that operate in a perfect market?
    I. Steel industry
    II. Agricultural commodities
    III. Banking services
    IV. Cleaning services
    V. Restaurants
    The CORRECT answer is:

    A. I, II, III
    B. I, II
    C. II, III, IV
    D. All of the above
    E. None of the above

27. There is still an overabundance of persons in the agricultural sector for all of the following reasons EXCEPT:

    A. Entry into certain occupations is blocked
    B. Migration is expensive
    C. Rents are low or non-existent
    D. Government subsidies counter price fluctuations
    E. Fear of the unknown

28. Which of the following are examples of oligopolies producing a homogeneous product?
    I. Steel industry
    II. Automobile industry
    III. OPEC
    IV. Soft drink industry
    V. Cigarette industry
    The CORRECT answer is:

    A. I, II, III
    B. I, II
    C. I, II, V
    D. I, III
    E. All of the above

29. Which of the following is TRUE of income distribution since World War II?

    A. Income has become less equally distributed.
    B. Income distribution has remained stable.
    C. Income has become more equally distributed.
    D. The percent in middle and upper income classes has decreased.
    E. The percent in lower, middle, and upper income classes has remained stable.

30. The profit of a firm is maximized when
    A. the market price of the factor is less than the value of the marginal physical product
    B. the market price of the factor is greater than the value of the marginal physical product
    C. the market price of the factor equals the value of the marginal physical product
    D. the hourly wage rate prevailing in the market decreases
    E. an increase in labor does not cause a decline in marginal revenue

31. All of the following are characteristics of poverty EXCEPT
    A. families in rural and agricultural areas
    B. non-white persons
    C. unskilled laborers
    D. elderly and disabled persons
    E. female heads of households

32. Which of the following are TRUE of changes in income and demand shifts?
    I. Income elasticity can change along the demand curve.
    II. Income elasticity can change with income.
    III. Income elasticity is positive.
    IV. Inferior commodities are inherently more price elastic than superior commodities.
    V. Nominal income elasticity can change with demand.
    The CORRECT answer is:
    A. I, III   B. I, II, III
    C. II, V   D. IV, V
    E. II, III, IV

33. Marginal revenue of a firm is
    A. less than the prevailing market price
    B. the same as the prevailing market price
    C. more than the prevailing market price
    D. set by how much the firm produces
    E. affected by other firms in the market

34. How does a market economy differ from a planned economy?
    I. Producers respond to consumer demand.
    II. Introduction of new techniques of production are slow.
    III. Equilibrium exists between supply and demand.
    IV. Price mechanism is very much limited.
    V. There is no need for planning committees to expand or contract industries.
    The CORRECT answer is:
    A. I, III, V   B. I, V
    C. I, II, V   D. I, II, III, V
    E. I, III, IV

35. What is the MAIN farm problem?
    A. Low productivity
    B. Rapid advance in productivity
    C. Surplus of human agents working on farms

D. Costly price support programs
E. Low price elasticity of the aggregate of agricultural goods

36. Antitrust laws have been MOST effective in cases involving   36.____

    A. mergers
    B. holding companies
    C. trusts
    D. use of patents
    E. price leadership

37. What are the MOST important factors determining the level of income of individuals?   37.____
    I. Industry
    II. The level of schooling
    III. The distribution of wealth among families
    IV. Area of specialization
    V. The flow from firms to families

    The CORRECT answer is:

    A. I, V
    B. I, II
    C. III, V
    D. II, III
    E. II, IV

38. Who are the *demanders of capital?*   38.____

    A. Laborers seeking increases in hourly wage rates
    B. Firms and individuals who decide to forego current consumption
    C. Firms who respond to rising costs by increasing the scale of production
    D. Corporations engaged in the production of machinery or equipment
    E. Entrepreneurs entering a high-risk enterprise

39. Microeconomic theory is based on the assumption that entrepreneurs are governed by   39.____

    A. satisfaction
    B. profit maximization
    C. the necessity of reaching a compromise among rival managerial units
    D. technology
    E. the net growth of active firms in the economy

40. All of the following market situations give rise to monopolies and oligopolies EXCEPT   40.____

    A. ownership of a patent
    B. requirement of a huge initial investment to enter the industry
    C. high overhead costs
    D. existence of an unlimited market
    E. a barrier of economic warfare

41. Anti-trust legislation is important MAINLY because of its   41.____

    A. role in defining illegalities
    B. preventative power
    C. punitive power
    D. role in eliminating monopolies
    E. economic power

42. Which of the following is an example of profits arising from the limited supply of specific resources?

    A. A patent for a particular process or product is held by one company
    B. Price escalation of crude oil by OPEC
    C. Farmland sold to commercial and residential land developers
    D. Medical school enrollment quotas
    E. A short supply of entrepreneurs willing to bear the high risks of a specific industry

43. Increases in prices and wages bring on an increase in all of the following EXCEPT the

    A. labor force
    B. supply of products
    C. suppliers of funds
    D. amount of cultivable land in production
    E. quantity of plant, machinery, and equipment supplies

44. If the price of another factor of production changes,

    A. it is uncertain whether the demand of the factor under consideration will be affected
    B. the demand for the factor under consideration will increase
    C. the demand for the factor under consideration will decrease
    D. the demand for the factor under consideration remains unchanged
    E. the demand for the factor under consideration will change to the same extent as all the other factors of production do

45. In a perfect market, the price of a commodity is

    A. determined by the existence of competition
    B. affected by the geographic location of the markets
    C. the same anywhere in the market
    D. altered by differences of services that are added to the product
    E. not subject to change

46. All of the following account for diminishing farm revenue EXCEPT:

    A. Movement of labor from the farm sector to the non-farm sector
    B. Slow increase in the demand for food
    C. Low income elasticity
    D. Low price elasticity of food
    E. Increases in farm output

47. In order for a cartel to be a monopoly, it
    I. must be an organization of a large number of firms established to sell and promote their product and to fix its price
    II. needs a strong form of organization
    III. must be able to allot quotas to its members
    IV. must have practically all producers organized into one cartel
    V. must be endorsed and enforced by the government

    The CORRECT answer is:

    A. I, II
    B. I, II, IV
    C. I, II, V
    D. II, III, IV
    E. All of the above

48. Taxes levied on the basis of the benefit principle include:
    I. Gasoline tax
    II. Cigarette tax
    III. Highway tolls
    IV. Liquor tax
    V. Hunting licenses
    The CORRECT answer is:

    A. I, II, IV
    B. I, III
    C. I, III, V
    D. II, IV, V
    E. All of the above

49. Which microeconomic problem is the MOST controversial?

    A. Cost of goods and services
    B. Quality of goods and services
    C. Rate of economic growth
    D. Regulation of prices
    E. Distribution of purchasing power

50. The number of hours worked per worker generally decreases with respect to

    A. changes in the hourly wage rate
    B. changes in population
    C. the level of education
    D. marginal cost increases
    E. technological advances

KEY (CORRECT ANSWERS)

1. A	11. E	21. E	31. C	41. B
2. B	12. C	22. A	32. B	42. C
3. A	13. D	23. E	33. B	43. A
4. B	14. F	24. C	34. A	44. A
5. A	15. A	25. D	35. C	45. C
6. B	16. D	26. C	36. E	46. A
7. C	17. C	27. D	37. D	47. D
8. D	18. C	28. D	38. B	48. C
9. C	19. C	29. C	39. B	49. E
10. E	20. B	30. C	40. D	50. A

EXAMINATION SECTION

TEST 1

DIRECTIONS: Each question or incomplete statement is followed by **several suggested answers or completions**. Select the one that BEST answers the question or completes the statement. *PRINT THE LETTER OF THE CORRECT ANSWER IN THE SPACE AT THE RIGHT.*

1. Which of the following statements is TRUE of government expenditures?
   The
   I. expenditures of state and local governments roughly equal those of the federal government
   II. federal government spends more on highways than state or local governments
   III. federal government spends less on education than state or local governments
   IV. main disadvantage of the three-level system of government is that local governments of poor areas lack financial leverage
   V. main advantage of the three-level system of government is that it has economic benefits
   The CORRECT answer is:
   A. I, III, V
   B. I, II, III
   C. I, IV, V
   D. II, III, IV
   E. I, III, IV

2. What is the rate structure of the personal income tax?
   A. Progressive
   B. Regressive
   C. Proportional
   D. Marginal
   E. Specific

3. All of the following are negative aspects of the United States tax program EXCEPT:
   A. The federal tax rate is not efficiently progressive.
   B. The tax structure favors certain groups
   C. State taxes are largely proportional.
   D. There is double taxation of corporation earnings.
   E. Excise taxes are not entirely based on the benefit principle.

4. The labor force participation rate has declined over the past hundred years among
   I. young people
   II. women
   III. minorities
   IV. older people
   V. farm workers
   The CORRECT answer is:
   A. I, V
   B. II, III
   C. II, III, IV
   D. IV, V
   E. I, IV, V

5. All of the following are functions of national unions EXCEPT to
   A. oversee local union activities
   B. police national unions against corruption
   C. assist the locals in bargaining and technical operations of the local
   D. stimulate and organize membership campaigns
   E. assist locals in labor-management disputes

6. How do economists judge the existence of tariffs? Tariffs
   A. are an important source of revenue
   B. protect our economy against cheap labor
   C. protect foreign economies against efficient American labor
   D. benefit only a few pressure groups
   E. create a large market for domestic commodities

7. What happens to farmers' incomes when there is a bad harvest? Incomes
   A. *fall*, because there is less to sell
   B. *fall*, because prices are low
   C. *fall*, because there is less demand
   D. *rise*, because the cost of the factors of production fall
   E. *rise*, because of the decrease in supply

8. Which of the following services do NOT enjoy "economies of scale" in the public sector?
   I. Schooling   II. Fire protection   III. Highways
   IV. Water   V. Sewage services
   The CORRECT answer is:
   A. I, II, V
   B. I, II
   C. I, II, IV
   D. III, IV, V
   E. III, IV

9. In terms of production, the length of the long run depends on
   A. output
   B. the industry under consideration
   C. the size of the factors of production
   D. the budget
   E. the production schedule

10. Monopolists make profits because
    A. the factors of production cost less
    B. they are protected by the government
    C. entry into the industry is blocked or restricted
    D. of efficient utilization of resources
    E. of price discrimination

11. Why would a monopolist lower the price of a commodity in a foreign market?
    A. Greater government regulations
    B. Price discrimination yields higher profits
    C. Demand is more elastic abroad
    D. Tariffs increase costs
    E. Lack of knowledge of the market

12. What is the relationship of firms in an oligopolistic market organization?
    A. Interlocking
    B. Complementary
    C. Mutually exclusive
    D. Purely competitive
    E. Mutually interdependent

13. The demand curve facing each oligopolist at the prevailing market price is
    A. kinked
    B. vertical
    C. horizontal
    D. positive
    E. negative

14. A market in which there is a single buyer of a resource is a(n)
    A. monopoly
    B. perfect monopoly
    C. natural monopoly
    D. monopsony
    E. oligopsony

15. What is considered the MAIN problem the public sector has now and will continue to have in the future?
    A. A large government deficit
    B. A budget that consists mostly of transfer payments
    C. Increased prices for goods and services
    D. Providing public services in the metropolitan area
    E. Providing public services in rural areas

16. Which of the following taxes are based on the benefit principle?
    I. Death and gift taxes
    II. Excise tax on gasoline
    III. Payroll taxes
    IV. Property taxes
    V. Personal income taxes
    The CORRECT answer is:
    A. I, III, IV
    B. I, III
    C. II, III, IV
    D. II, V
    E. II, IV

17. The potential of the economy to produce is determined by
    I. the size of the labor force
    II. the accumulation of capital
    III. political bias
    IV. the state of technology
    V. balance of payments deficit
    The CORRECT answer is:
    A. I, III, IV
    B. I, II, IV
    C. I, IV, V
    D. I, II, III
    E. I, III, V

18. The labor force is the
    A. number of people working more than fifteen hours a week
    B. number of persons employed and unemployed who are sixteen-years-old and older
    C. United States population over sixteen years of age who are not disabled
    D. number of people engaged in productive activity regardless of age, race, or sex
    E. population over eighteen years of age who are not disabled

19. When an employee changes employers, for example, leaves Ford to go to Chrysler, the move is called
    A. interfirm
    B. interindustry
    C. labor force attachment
    D. intrafirm
    E. structural

20. Why is it so difficult to equalize differences in wages? Because
    A. of skill requirements associated with each job
    B. of job shortages
    C. of nonpecuniary benefits associated with each job
    D. most workers are unionized
    E. our economy is based on capitalism

21. What CHIEFLY distinguishes international trade from domestic trade?
    A. Goods and services cross a border or frontier
    B. Tariffs and quotas are imposed
    C. The exchange of goods is regulated by governments
    D. The type of goods and services that are exchanged.
    E. The type of currency used to settle debts

22. Why is the American economy considered to be a "mixed" economy? Because
    A. there are various socio-economic classes
    B. of the interaction between skilled and unskilled laborers
    C. it does not have monopolies
    D. both public and private institutions exercise economic control
    E. it is based on theories of capitalism

23. Which of the following is TRUE of marginal utility and consumer consumption? Marginal utility is
    A. *positive* but declines as long as total utility rises
    B. *positive* when total utility is neither rising nor falling
    C. *negative* at the saturation point
    D. *zero* as long a total utility is rising
    E. *zero* as long as total utility is falling

24. Perfect competition is MOST probably among
    A. soft drink manufacturers
    B. certain clothing items
    C. automobiles
    D. certain agricultural commodities
    E. canned and frozen goods

25. What is the relationship between pure monopoly and perfect competition?
    A. Opposite
    B. Complementary
    C. Synonymous
    D. Interdependent
    E. Independent

26. Differentiated oligopolies are industries producing
    I.   cement   II. cigarettes   III. steel
    IV. automobiles   V. aluminum
    The CORRECT answer is:
    A. I, III, V   B. III, IV, V   C. II, IV
    D. All of the above E. None of the above

27. All of the following are obstacles to collusion EXCEPT
    A. price wars   B. antitrust laws
    C. poor economic conditions D. product differentiation
    E. large numbers of firms

28. What is the MAIN difference between craft unions and industrial unions?
    A. Tactics   B. Effectiveness
    C. Benefits   D. Membership
    E. There is no difference

29. Which of the following taxes is recessive? _____ tax
    A. Excise   B. Ad Valorem   C. Sales
    D. Estate   E. Personal income

30. What are the *positive* aspects of the tax structure in the United States?
    I.   The Federal income tax is effectively progressive.
    II. The various levels of government collect far more money than is earned in most nations.
    III. The tax structure is largely impartial.
    IV. A relatively small proportion of resources is required for the collection of taxes.
    V.   The tax system is a stabilizing feature of the economy.
    The CORRECT answer is:
    A. I, III, V   B. I, II, IV   C. II, III
    D. II, IV, V   E. II, III, V

31. The wage rate is determined by the
    A. cost of living
    B. price index
    C. supply and demand for labor
    D. stabilization factors operating in the economy
    E. factors of production

32. Which of the following is TRUE of new technology? It
    A. causes real wages to rise
    B. decreases the demand for labor
    C. reduces the accumulation of capital
    D. is labor-absorbing with respect to skilled and professional labor
    E. compels management to use their workers more efficiently

33. The fundamental basis of the union is to
    A. raise wages
    B. police employers
    C. manipulate the economy
    D. provide more economic power for workers
    E. regulate the supply of labor in the economy

34. Anyone who buys or sells a good in large enough quantities to be **able to affect** the price of that good is termed a(n)
    A. imperfect competitor
    B. perfect competitor
    C. monopolist
    D. price leader
    E. consumer

35. **The actual** out-of-pocket expenditures of the firm required to purchase or hire the services of the factors of production it needs are called _____ costs.
    A. explicit
    B. implicit
    C. opportunity
    D. total
    E. total fixed

36. **All of the** following may result in a pure monopoly EXCEPT
    A. increasing returns to scale
    B. control over the supply of raw materials
    C. efficient utilization of resources
    D. patents
    E. government franchise

37. What is the BASIC difference between the perfectly competitive firm and the monopolist when the latter does not affect factor prices?
    A. Production
    B. Cost
    C. Demand
    D. Supply
    E. Price

38. What is the MOST prevalent form of market organization in retailing?
    A. Pure monopoly
    B. Natural monopoly
    C. Oligopoly
    D. Monopolistic competition
    E. Perfect competition

39. Why do oligopolists rarely engage in price competition?
    A. Fear of government intervention
    B. Fear of triggering a price war
    C. Fear of their reputation
    D. The product is homogeneous
    E. There are too few sellers in the market

40. What are the MOST important sources of revenue for the state government?
    I. Corporation income taxes
    II. Personal income taxes
    III. Sales taxes
    IV. Excise taxes
    V. Death and gift taxes
    The CORRECT answer is:
    A. I, II   B. II, IV   C. II, III   D. III, IV   E. III, V

41. An example of a capital gain is the difference between
    A. what a retailer buys merchandise for and what the item is sold for
    B. the selling price of an item and the total price
    C. a corporation's accounts payable and accounts receivable
    D. the purchase price of stock and the selling price
    E. the current assets of a corporation and its current liabilities

42. Which of the following is an example of interindustry mobility? When an employee
    A. moves from one employer to another
    B. switches from one skill area to another
    C. changes his labor force status
    D. goes from one firm to another within the same industry
    E. shifts industrial sectors

43. Which of the following statements are TRUE of tariffs as a source of revenue?
    I. Tariffs are an important source of revenue for the government.
    II. A tariff is a regressive tax.
    III. Tariffs are not imposed according to the benefit principle.
    IV. Tariffs are conducive to higher domestic wages which indirectly increase government revenue.
    V. Tariffs cause a significant loss of welfare to both countries involved.
    The CORRECT answer is:
    A. I, III, V
    B. II, III, V
    C. I, III, IV
    D. II, IV, V
    E. III, IV, V

44. Consumer's equilibrium is the point at which the
    A. consumer's disposable income equals consumption
    B. consumer's disposable income intersects the consumer's demand schedule
    C. price of items of consumption equals what the consumer is willing to pay for them
    D. consumer maximizes the total utility of satisfaction from spending his income
    E. consumer's demand is met by the supply of goods and services available

45. What are *implicit costs*? The
    A. actual out-of-pocket expenditures of the firm to purchase or hire the services of the factors of production it needs
    B. cost to society incurred by the use of diminishing natural resources
    C. costs of the services of the factors owned and used by the firm in its own production process
    D. costs which the firm incurs in the short-run for all fixed inputs
    E. sum of total fixed costs less explicit costs

46. Generally, if a monopolist wants to swell more of a commodity, 46.____
    A. additional factors of production must be employed
    B. quality must be increased
    C. it must be advertised
    D. production must increase
    E. the price must be lowered

47. How does a natural monopoly DIFFER from a pure monopoly? 47.____
    A. It operates under a government franchise.
    B. It is subject to government regulation.
    C. It is able to satisfy the entire market at a lower per-unit cost than two or more firms could.
    D. It does not block the entry of competing firms
    E. None of the above

48. Which of the following are examples of monopolistic competition? 48.____
    I.   Public transportation   II. Electrical companies
    III. Telephone companies   IV. Gasoline stations
    V.   Grocery stores
    The CORRECT answer is:
    A. I, II, III   B. II, III   C. II, III, IV
    D. IV, V   E. I, II, III, IV

49. Which of the following is TRUE of price leadership? It 49.____
    A. is illegal
    B. is a form of price discrimination
    C. is a form of tacit collusion
    D. is a form of overt collusion
    E. signifies a centralized cartel

50. Real wages have risen in the United States over time because 50.____
    A. labor has become the most important resource
    B. the general price level has risen
    C. the productivity of labor has increased
    D. of the effect of unions on wages
    E. of the growth of imperfect competition in the market

KEY (CORRECT ANSWERS)

1.	E	11.	C	21.	A	31.	C	41.	D
2.	A	12.	E	22.	E	32.	D	42.	E
3.	C	13.	A	23.	A	33.	D	43.	B
4.	E	14.	D	24.	D	34.	A	44.	D
5.	B	15.	D	25.	A	35.	A	45.	C
6.	D	16.	C	26.	C	36.	C	46.	E
7.	E	17.	B	27.	A	37.	C	47.	E
8.	B	18.	B	28.	D	38.	D	48.	D
9.	B	19.	A	29.	A	39.	B	49.	C
10.	C	20.	C	30.	D	40.	D	50.	C

EXAMINATION SECTION
TEST 1

DIRECTIONS: Each question or incomplete statement is followed by several suggested answers or completions. Select the one that BEST answers the question or completes the statement. *PRINT THE LETTER OF THE CORRECT ANSWER IN THE SPACE AT THE RIGHT.*

1. The demand for labor is a(n) _____ demand.   1.____
   A. empirical
   B. artificial
   C. marginal
   D. derived
   E. quantitative

2. What is the MAIN source of revenue for the Federal government?   2.____
   A. Property taxes
   B. Sales taxes
   C. Tariffs
   D. Excise taxes
   E. Personal income taxes

3. Which of the following are TRUE of an ad valorem tax? It is   3.____
   I.   a tax in which a certain percentage of the price is paid on each unit
   II. based on the benefits principle
   III. a specific tax
   IV. an excise tax
   V.   a progressive tax
   The CORRECT answer is:
   A. I, IV
   B. I, III, IV
   C. I, IV, V
   D. II, III
   E. I, V

4. Which of the following taxation guidelines resulted from the experience of the Great Depression?   4.____
   I.   Taxes should be direct.
   II. The government should not overburden the people with taxes.
   III. Taxes should not be arbitrary.
   IV. Interference with economic incentives should be minimized.
   V.   The tax base should be broad.
   The CORRECT answer is:
   A. I, IV, V
   B. I, II, III
   C. I, II, V
   D. I, III
   E. III, IV, V

5. Which of the following are TRUE of the long-run supply of labor?   5.____
   There has been a(n)
   I.   decrease in the demand for labor
   II. steady increase in the population
   III. unchanged aggregate labor-force participation rate
   IV. decline in hours worked per worker
   V.   increase in the unemployment rate
   The CORRECT answer is:
   A. I, II, V
   B. II, V
   C. II, III, IV
   D. I, III, IV
   E. I, IV, V

21

2 (#1)

6. All of the following are functions of the AFL-CIO EXCEPT: 6.____
   A. Educate workers in unionism
   B. Lobby for labor's political interest in Congress
   C. Settle disputes among various national unions
   D. Research activities relevant to economic issues should be pursued
   E. Bargain with employers over conditions of employment

7. What is the MAIN objection to a minimum wage? It 7.____
   A. reduces productivity
   B. causes the demand curve to shift upward
   C. creates an unemployment problem
   D. undermines union influence
   E. is inflationary

8. All of the following problems are common and basic to all economies EXCEPT: 8.____
   A. What commodities shall be produced
   B. In what quantities shall commodities be produced
   C. How shall goods be produced
   D. For whom should goods be produced
   E. What value shall be placed on goods that are produced

9. What is MOST likely to occur when the price of coffee falls? 9.____
   A. The price of complementary commodities rises.
   B. The price of complementary commodities falls.
   C. Consumers substitute coffee for tea in consumption.
   D. Consumers substitute tea for coffee in consumption.
   E. It has little effect on consumers' choice of tea or coffee.

10. Marginal utility explains the price difference consumers are willing to pay for 10.____
    A. soda and beer   B. milk and gold
    C. cigarettes and fuel oil   D. a pencil and a typewriter
    E. water and electricity

11. Perfectly competitive products compete in terms of 11.____
    I.   service   II. advertising and promotion
    III. quality   IV. style
    V.   price
    The CORRECT answer is:
    A. I, V   B. II, V   C. I, III, V
    D. All of the above   E. None of the above

12. What limits the market power of pure monopolists? Fear of 12.____
    I.   substitute commodities   II. government prosecution
    III. the threat of potential competitors   IV. changing consumer tastes
    V.   changes in consumer incomes
    The CORRECT answer is:
    A. I, II, III   B. II, IV, V   C. II, IV
    D. All of the above   E. None of the above

13. The monopolistic competitor CHIEFLY engages in
    A. Price competition
    B. Non-price competition
    C. Price leadership
    D. Price discrimination
    E. Eliminating competition by blocking or restricting entry of competitors

14. The MOST prevalent form of market organization in the manufacturing sector of modern economies is
    A. pure monopoly
    B. natural monopoly
    C. monopolistic competition
    D. oligopoly
    E. perfect competition

15. Where is a monopsont MOST likely to occur? In a(n)
    A. rural area
    B. suburban area
    C. urban area
    D. remote village
    E. small industrial town

16. How does the national income accounts budget differ from the administrative budget? It includes
    A. the purchases of goods and services
    B. income and expenditures from government-controlled trust funds
    C. transfer payments
    D. all revenues to be made on the basis of congressional action
    E. exhaustive expenditures

17. Which of the following are considered progressive taxes?
    I.   Death and gift taxes
    II. Ad valorem tax
    III. Sales tax
    IV. Personal income tax
    V.   Excise tax
    The CORRECT answer is:
    A. I, III, IV
    B. I, II, IV
    C. III, IV, V
    D. II, III, IV
    E. III, IV

18. All of the following are true of a *negative income tax* program EXCEPT:
    A. It is derived from the idea of a guaranteed annual income.
    B. The amount is determined by the level of income and the number of exemptions.
    C. It is a way of dispensing funds without humiliating recipients.
    D. It is a viable alternative to the current welfare and farm price-support programs.
    E. It provides a strong work incentive to the poor and the unemployed.

19. The supply of labor is determined MAINLY by the
    I.   change in the size of the population, sixteen years and over
    II. change in technology
    III. labor-force participation rate
    IV. increases in the immigrant population sixteen years and over
    V.   number of man-hours offered by each worker per annum

The CORRECT answer is:
A. I, II
B. I, II, IV
C. II, III, IV
D. I, III, V
E. I, III, IV

20. Which of the following is an example of interoccupational mobility? When a worker
    A. moves from the New York to the Chicago branch of his firm
    B. goes from Ford to General Motors
    C. advances from advertising executive to the head of sales
    D. goes from Ford to United Airlines
    E. quits a job to return to school for new training

21. What does the additional *worker hypothesis* suggest about the labor force?
    A. Individuals enter the labor force when employment opportunities exist.
    B. There is hidden unemployment during recessions.
    C. There are more laborers working fewer hours when wages are high.
    D. When wages are high, there are fewer secondary workers in the labor market.
    E. There are more secondary workers when primary wage earners become unemployed during slack periods.

22. How does a free trade area DIFFER from a common market?
    A. Members eliminate trade barriers among themselves.
    B. Members are able to exclude certain commodities from the free trade agreement.
    C. Members are free to set up a common external wall of tariffs.
    D. There is free movement of manpower and capital among the members.
    E. Members are free to set differing tariffs and quotas on goods imported from the rest of the world.

23. Why is a supply curve usually positively sloped?
    A. More of a commodity will be supplied at lower prices.
    B. Less of a commodity will be supplied at higher prices.
    C. More of a commodity will be supplied at higher prices.
    D. Price and quantity are inversely related along a supply curve.
    E. More of a commodity will be supplied when the price of other commodities related in production remain unchanged.

24. What is the average fixed cost?
    A. Total costs divided by output
    B. Total variable costs divided by output
    C. Total fixed costs divided by output
    D. The sum of total fixed costs and total variable costs
    E. The costs which the firm incurs in the short-run for all fixed inputs, regardless of the level of output

25. Which of the following are examples of fixed factors of production in the short-run?
    I. Payments for renting land and buildings
    II. Insurance
    III. Property taxes
    IV. Cost of fuels
    V. Excise taxes
    The CORRECT answer is:
    A. I, III, V
    B. I, II, III, V
    C. I, II, III
    D. I, III, IV, V
    E. All of the above

26. A fuel oil company charges less per gallon for more volume. This is an example of
    A. increasing returns to scale
    B. opportunity cost
    C. average variable cost
    D. price discrimination
    E. long-run pricing

27. Why is the demand for the monopolist's product more elastic abroad?
    A. Less government regulation
    B. More government regulation
    C. Less competition
    D. More competition
    E. More demand

28. Oligopolists are NOT likely to compete on the basis of
    A. quality
    B. product design
    C. price
    D. customer service
    E. advertising

29. What does the kinked-demand curve model explain in reference to oligopolistic market?
    A. How prices react
    B. Price decreases
    C. Price increases
    D. How prevailing prices were determined
    E. Price rigidity

30. All of the following are true EXCEPT:
    A. Firms demand resources because of the utility or satisfaction they get from them.
    B. The more productive a resource is in producing a commodity, the greater the resource price.
    C. Firms demand resources in order to produce goods and services demanded by consumers.
    D. The price of resources is determined by its market demand and supply.
    E. Consumers demand final commodities because of the utility or satisfaction they get from them.

31. The growth of government transfer payments reflect a
    A. growth of the public sector
    B. shift of the age factor in the population
    C. social trend to increase the purchasing power of the needy
    D. political trend to increase the purchasing power of the needy
    E. decrease in purchases of goods and services

31.____

32. What is a *specific tax*?
    A. A tax placed on a specific item of purchase
    B. A tax placed on a specific type of business
    C. A specific percentage tax on certain items of purchase
    D. A specific amount of tax money due per unit regardless of the value of the commodity
    E. A specific amount of tax money due on personal incomes that exceed a certain fixed index

32.____

33. What are the weaknesses in the United States tax structure?
    I.   The depletion allowance is discriminatory.
    II. The tax base of many states and localities is not growing with their needs.
    III. There are too many taxes at all levels that are confusing to the public.
    IV. The overall system is regressive.
    V.   A large portion of our resources is used inefficiently to collect taxes.
    The CORRECT answer is:
    A. I, II, IV   B. I, II, III   C. II, III
    D. II, III, V   E. II, IV, V

33.____

34. Why is the supply of labor upward sloping? Because at a
    A. higher wage rate, firms are ready to employ more labor
    B. higher daily wage rate, the quality of labor increases
    C. higher daily wage rate, more man-days are offered in the labor market
    D. lower wage rate, entrepreneurs substitute labor for capital
    E. lower wage rate, entrepreneurs expand their scale of operations

34.____

35. Why has there been an increase in the labor-force participation rate of women?
    I.   Women have been receiving more education
    II. Male prejudice has lessened
    III. The changing structure of industry toward jobs which females typically undertake
    IV. Increased salaries have lured women from the home
    V.   An increased demand for leisure by male workers opens many job opportunities
    The CORRECT answer is:
    A. I, II, III   B. I, IV   C. I, IV, V
    D. I, II, IV   E. All of the above

35.____

36. All of the following are functions of local unions EXCEPT:
    A. Bargain with employers over wages, hours, and conditions of employment
    B. Handle grievances under the contract
    C. Serve as the national union's eyes and ears
    D. Collect dues and increase membership
    E. Organize social functions

37. Malthus' theory of population rests on the law of
    A. increasing relative costs
    B. wages
    C. diminishing returns
    D. supply and demand
    E. optimum population

38. Consumer's surplus refers to the differences between
    A. personal disposable income and total demand
    B. personal disposable income and the cost of necessities
    C. personal income and personal income taxes
    D. what the consumer would be willing to pay for a give quantity of a commodity and what he actually pays
    E. the consumer's anticipated demand during a certain given period of time and the amount of actual consumption

39. The costs which the firm incurs in the short run for all fixed inputs, regardless of the level of output, is termed
    A. long-run marginal cost
    B. long-run average cost
    C. total cost
    D. total variable costs
    E. total fixed costs

40. All of the following are advantages of perfect competition EXCEPT:
    A. Resources are efficiently utilized
    B. Social costs are reduced
    C. Consumers pay lower prices
    D. In long-run equilibrium, firms operate at the optimum scale of the plant and level of output
    E. The forces of competition eliminate all profits in the long run

41. How is the demand curve for a monopolist's commodity sloped?
    A. Positively
    B. Negatively
    C. Horizontally
    D. Vertically
    E. Upward and downward

42. Which of the following is NOT true of a pure monopolist in the United States?
    A. Government regulation
    B. Relatively uncommon in numbers
    C. Unlimited market power
    D. Indirect competition for the consumer's dollar from all other commodities
    E. Threat of potential competition

43. The existence of monopolies tends to increase income inequality because
    A. corporate stocks are owned mostly by high-income groups
    B. competition is non-existent
    C. prices are high
    D. of price discrimination
    E. demand is inelastic

44. The demand curve for commodities of the monopolistic competitor is negatively sloped because of
    A. product differentiation
    B. the availability of close substitutes
    C. price competition
    D. non-price competition
    E. price rigidity

45. The monopolistic competitor faces a demand curve that is
    A. positively sloped
    B. horizontally sloped
    C. highly inelastic
    D. highly elastic
    E. infinitely elastic

46. Does the *perfect competitor* engage in non-price competition?
    A. *Yes*, to convince customers that its product is superior
    B. *Yes*, to convince customers that its price is lowest.
    C. *Yes*, to educate consumers and inform them of new products
    D. *No*, because the homogeneity of the product allows sales of any quantity at the prevailing market price
    E. *No*, because it adds to costs that are passed on to consumers

47. A firm's demand for a productive resource will increase for all of the following reasons EXCEPT the
    A. product demand increases
    B. total revenue decreases
    C. productivity of the resources rises
    D. prices of complementary resources fall
    E. prices of substitute resources rise

48. The demand for loanable funds is _____ sloped.
    A. positively
    B. negatively
    C. horizontally
    D. vertically
    E. variably

49. What is the MAIN source of revenue of local governments?
    A. Death and gift taxes
    B. Property taxes
    C. Sales taxes
    D. Excise taxes
    E. Payroll taxes

50. All of the following are maxims formulated by Adam Smith for imposing taxes EXCEPT that the
    A. taxes should be proportional to the ability to pay
    B. taxes should be administered to stabilize the economy
    C. taxes should not be arbitrary
    D. timing of levying taxes should be convenient to the contributor
    E. government should not overburden the people with taxes

50._____

KEY (CORRECT ANSWERS)

1.	D	11.	E	21.	E	31.	C	41.	B
2.	E	12.	A	22.	E	32.	D	42.	C
3.	A	13.	B	23.	C	33.	B	43.	A
4.	A	14.	D	24.	C	34.	C	44.	A
5.	C	15.	E	25.	C	35.	A	45.	D
6.	E	16.	B	26.	D	36.	A	46.	D
7.	C	17.	B	27.	D	37.	C	47.	B
8.	E	18.	E	28.	C	38.	D	48.	B
9.	C	19.	D	29.	E	39.	E	49.	B
10.	B	20.	C	30.	A	40.	B	50.	B

EXAMINATION SECTION
TEST 1

DIRECTIONS: Each question or incomplete statement is followed by several suggested answers or completions. Select the one that BEST answers the question or completes the statement. *PRINT THE LETTER OF THE CORRECT ANSWER IN THE SPACE AT THE RIGHT.*

1. The disadvantages of a monopoly are:
    I. Resources are misallocated
    II. Monopoly profits lead to greater income inequity
    III. Due to security in the market, there may be little research and development
    IV. Smaller quantities are produced
    V. Price discrimination exists

    The *correct* answer is:

    A. I, V
    B. III, IV, V
    C. II, V
    D. I, IV
    E. All of the above

1.____

2. Which of the following occupational groups are non-competing?
    I. Porters
    II. Garbage collectors
    III. Shoemakers
    IV. Car washers
    V. Engineers

    The *correct* answer is:

    A. I, II, IV
    B. I, III, V
    C. III, V
    D. All of the above
    E. None of the above

2.____

3. Complete specialization refers to

    A. a nation which produces only one of the two commodities which trade
    B. the ability of a nation to produce a commodity at a relatively lower cost than another nation
    C. an economy which has no trade or financial relationships with the rest of the world
    D. a two-nation, two-commodity world
    E. none of the above

3.____

4. The flows of goods, services, and government grants between the nation and the rest of the world is shown in the

    A. Capital Account
    B. Current Account
    C. Annual Trade Account
    D. Official Reserve Account
    E. Offical Trade Account

4.____

5. What determines the demand for land? The
   I. demand for the commodities that use land in production
   II. productivity of the land
   III. price for the use of land
   IV. market supply of land
   V. price of substitute resources

   The *correct* answer is :

   A. I, II, III
   B. III, IV
   C. I, II, III, IV
   D. II, III, IV
   E. I, II, V

6. Why do firms demand labor? To

   A. produce the products demanded by customers
   B. lessen unemployment
   C. realize full employment in the economy
   D. provide for the public good
   E. make a profit

7. What is the SINGLE characteristic that sets oligopoly apart from other market structures? The

   A. relationship among the firms in the industry
   B. factors that give rise to its existence
   C. type of firms in the industry
   D. control the government exerts on this form of market organization
   E. number of buyers for the commodities being sold

8. How does the government redistribute income from the rich to the poor? Through

   A. built-in stabilizers
   B. a system of rebates
   C. price and rent controls
   D. transfer payments
   E. a system of progressive taxation and subsidies

9. Most nations of the world have a (n) _____ economy.

   A. non-trading
   B. barter
   C. open
   D. closed
   E. specialized

10. What was the FUNDAMENTAL reason for the collapse of the Fixed Exchange Rate System? It

    A. resulted in erratic and unwanted fluctuations in exchange rates
    B. restricted trade
    C. allowed nations to keep their exchange rates artificially high in order to discourage imports
    D. resulted in a decline in the volume of, and gains from, trade and a loss to all nations
    E. lacked adequate adjustment mechanisms

11. The total supply of money is determined by   11.____

    A. demand
    B. the Federal Government
    C. commercial banks
    D. the level of National Income
    E. the GNP

12. All of the following are examined by resource pricing EXCEPT the determination of   12.____

    A. the wages of various kinds of labor
    B. consumer demand
    C. the rents of various types of land
    D. interest rates on capital assets
    E. profits from various forms of entrepreneurial activity

13. Non-competing occupational groups receive different wages because of   13.____

    A. differences among industries in the market
    B. job requirements
    C. equalizing differences
    D. imperfections in the labor market
    E. the supply of, and demand for, labor

14. All of the following account for international trade EXCEPT   14.____

    A. comparative advantage
    B. increasing returns to scale
    C. increasing costs
    D. differences in taste
    E. differences in resources

15. Which of the following industries/products would MOST LIKELY favor import tariffs and   15.____
    quotas?
    I. Automobile
    II. Agriculture
    III. Aircraft
    IV. Steel
    V. Textile
    The CORRECT answer is:

    A. I, IV
    B. I, II, III
    C. I, II, IV
    D. I, IV, V
    E. All of the above

16. Profits are MOST LIKELY to be the result of   16.____

    A. the introduction of new products
    B. monopoly power
    C. risky ventures
    D. shifting resources to the production of those commodities that society wants most
    E. efficiency and innovation

17. Which of the following are risks in economics?
    I. The breakdown of a machine
    II. A fall in revenue
    III. A fire
    IV. An increase in cost
    V. Theft

    The CORRECT answer is:

    A. II, III, IV, V
    B. II, V
    C. III, V
    D. I, III, V
    E. All of the above

18. Why is labor the MOST IMPORTANT resource?

    A. The welfare of the nation depends on it
    B. The supply is limited
    C. Each additional unit employed adds more to the firm's total revenue than to its total costs
    D. Its productivity exceeds that of other resources
    E. It represents the highest percent of the national income

19. What are wage differences based on?
    I. Equalizing differences
    II. Age and sex discrimination
    III. The existence of non-competing occupational groups
    IV. Union power
    V. Imperfections of competition in the labor markets

    The CORRECT answer is:

    A. I, II, IV
    B. I, III, V
    C. I, II, III
    D. I, III, IV
    E. All of the above

20. What is the result of trade restrictions in the U.S.A.?

    A. Labor is protected against cheap foreign labor
    B. Unemployment is reduced
    C. Infant industries are protected
    D. Prices rise and the range of goods is reduced
    E. Industry is forced to specialize in the production of the commodity with the higher opportunity cost

21. Which of the following is TRUE?

    A. The more developed a nation is, the larger its economic interdependence with the rest of the world
    B. The less developed a nation is, the smaller its economic interdependence with the rest of the world
    C. The larger the nation, the smaller its economic interdependence with the rest of the world
    D. The smaller the nation, the smaller its economic interdependence with the rest of the world
    E. Size or development does not affect a nation's economic interdependence with the rest of the world

22. Which of the following represents the LARGEST percentage of the U.S. National Income?

    A. Wages and salaries
    B. Proprietors' incomes
    C. Corporate profits
    D. Interest
    E. Rents

23. In general, the interest rate on a loan is higher WHEN
    I. there is a greater risk of borrower default
    II. the term of the loan is short
    III. the amount of the loan is small
    IV. the financial system is not competitive
    V. the pure interest rate rises

    The CORRECT answer is:

    A. I, V
    B. I, II, III
    C. I, IV, V
    D. I, III, V
    E. All of the above

24. The market supply of labor does NOT depend on the

    A. population size
    B. proportion of the population in the labor force
    C. state of the economy
    D. productivity of labor
    E. level of real wages

25. What are equalizing differences in wage determination?

    A. Fringe benefits offered by firms to attract workers
    B. Commissions offered to salesmen to compensate productivity
    C. Additional per-hour wage rate for overtime labor
    D. Higher wages for jobs requiring equal qualifications but differing in attractiveness
    E. Higher wages for workers who have remained with the firm for a fixed period of time

26. A measure of the degree of interdependence of a nation with the rest of the world is given by

    A. a statement of all transactions with the rest of the world during the year
    B. the value of its exports as a percentage of its GNP
    C. the flow of investments and loans between the nation and the rest of the world
    D. an account of the export of goods, services, and capital inflows
    E. an account of the flow of goods, services, and government grants between the nation and the rest of the world

27. The change in the nation's official reserves and liabilities needed to balance Current and Capital Accounts is shown in the

    A. Balance of Payments
    B. Balance of Trade
    C. Annual Trade Account
    D. Official Reserve Account
    E. Official Trade Account

28. Who is responsible for the tax on land?

    A. Land agents
    B. Land users
    C. Land owners
    D. Both land owners and users
    E. It varies according to local practice and law

29. What is a pure rate of interest? The

    A. price paid for the use of money
    B. fixed rate of interest on all loanable funds
    C. average of all interest rates during a fixed period of time
    D. rate of interest on riskless loans
    E. rate of interest on long-term government loans

30. What is the *MOST COMMON* method that unions use to increase workers' wages?

    A. Bargaining with employers under threat of a strike
    B. Financing advertising of union-made products
    C. Lobbying to restrict imports
    D. Restricting the supply of labor through high initiation fees and long apprenticeships
    E. Increasing labor productivity

31. Why will the marginal revenue product of a perfect competitor in the product market decline? Because of

    A. a declining commodity price
    B. a declining marginal physical product
    C. declining marginal revenue
    D. declining marginal physical product and the commodity price
    E. declining resource pricing

32. Equalizing differences exist in wage determination because

    A. of skill differences among employees
    B. of sex and age differences among employees
    C. of non-monetary differences among jobs
    D. of the imperfections of competition in labor markets
    E. there are non-competing occupational groups in the labor market

33. Under the Bretton Woods System, there is a

    A. fixed exchange rate system
    B. flexible exchange rate system
    C. floating exchange rate system
    D. depreciation of foreign currency during exchanges
    E. constant rate of exchange

34. Which of the following is TRUE of the United States and international trade? The

    A. USA has no need to trade
    B. size of the USA population forces us to trade
    C. basis of USA trade is political rather than economic

D. standard of living in the USA would be seriously affected without trade
E. disadvantages of trade outweigh the benefits for the USA

35. What is the MAIN purpose of the Balance of Payments? To help the government

   A. formulate monetary policy
   B. formulate fiscal policy
   C. formulate commercial policy
   D. plan economic strategy for the following year
   E. to understand the nation's international position.

36. A nation's demand for a foreign currency is, generally,

   A. upsloped
   B. downsloped
   C. vertically sloped
   D. U-sloped
   E. upsloped and kinked

37. In order to maximize profits, a firm borrows

   A. at the lowest interest rate
   B. when the interest rate is stable
   C. until the return on investment exceeds the rate of interest
   D. until the return on investment equals the rate of interest
   E. until the return on investment is smaller than the rate of interest

38. Why have proprietors' incomes declined over the years while wages and salaries have risen? The number of
   I. unionized labor has *increased*
   II. small, independent farmers has *declined*
   III. self-employed has *declined*
   IV. partnerships has *increased*
   V. corporations has *increased*

   The *CORRECT* answer is:

   A. I, II, V
   B. I, III, IV, V
   C. I, V
   D. II, V
   E. II, III, V

39. Market imperfections that cause wage differences include all of the following *EXCEPT*

   A. varying attractiveness of different jobs
   B. lack of information
   C. minimum wage laws
   D. union power
   E. unwillingness to move

40. Why do national monetary authorities intervene in foreign exchange markets? To

   A. prevent inflation and possible recession
   B. control large and chronic deficits
   C. control increases in the domestic currency price
   D. control trade and payments
   E. prevent erratic and unwanted fluctuations in exchange rates

41. The summary record of all the transactions of a nation with the rest of the world during a calendar year is called the

    A. Balance of Trade
    B. Balance of Payments
    C. Capital Account
    D. Current Account
    E. Annual Trade Account

42. The demand for loanable funds is _____ sloped.

    A. negatively
    B. vertically
    C. horizontally
    D. U-
    E. positively

43. Why have some economists thought that government revenues could be raised by taxing only rental incomes?

    A. The demand for land is infinitely elastic
    B. The supply of land is less than the demand for it
    C. The demand for land is constant
    D. The amount of land available is fixed
    E. Land is a more variable resource than either labor or capital

44. An "invention" refers to a (n)
    I. innovation
    II. new custom
    III. new process
    IV. new technique
    V. new product

The CORRECT answer is:

    A. I, III, IV
    B. II, III, IV
    C. III, IV, V
    D. I, V
    E. II, III, IV, V

45. How does the government seek to overcome the distortions resulting from market imperfections? Through

    A. the Federal Reserve System
    B. transfer payments
    C. a system of taxes and controls
    D. built-in stabilizers
    E. fiscal policy

46. All of the following are major international economic problems facing the world today EXCEPT:

    A. Worldwide inflation and the possibility of recession
    B. Huge balance-of-payment deficits in most petroleum-exporting nations
    C. An inadequate international monetary system
    D. The lack of national and international controls to regulate corporations operating outside the jurisdiction of any one nation
    E. Lagging economic development in the world's poor nations

47. Which of the following is NOT entered as a debit in the accounts of the Balance of Payments?

A. USA import of goods and services
B. Government grants made to foreigners
C. Investments received from abroad
D. Loans made to foreigners
E. Investments made to foreigners

48. What is an interest rate?

    A. The price of exchanging money for goods
    B. The price of using money or loanable funds
    C. A percentage of the total of loanable funds
    D. A percentage of the money used by borrowers
    E. A price determined by the supply of loanable funds

49. An upward shift in the supply curve is the result of a tax on
    I. wages
    II. salaries
    III. land
    IV. natural resources
    V. interest income

    The CORRECT answer is:

    A. I, II
    B. I, II, V
    C. I, II, III, V
    D. III, IV
    E. All of the above

50. The level of real wages depends on

    A. the technology of production
    B. the state of the economy
    C. actual purchasing power
    D. the amount of capital available per worker
    E. the productivity of labor

KEY (CORRECT ANSWERS)

1. E	11. B	21. C	31. B	41. B
2. D	12. B	22. A	32. C	42. A
3. A	13. B	23. C	33. A	43. D
4. B	14. C	24. D	34. D	44. C
5. E	15. D	25. D	35. E	45. C
6. A	16. B	26. B	36. B	46. B
7. A	17. D	27. D	37. D	47. C
8. E	18. E	28. C	38. E	48. B
9. C	19. B	29. D	39. A	49. B
10. E	20. D	30. A	40. E	50. E

EXAMINATION SECTION
TEST 1

DIRECTIONS: Each question or incomplete statement is followed by several suggested answers or completions. Select the one that BEST answers the question or completes the statement. *PRINT THE LETTER OF THE CORRECT ANSWER IN THE SPACE AT THE RIGHT.*

1.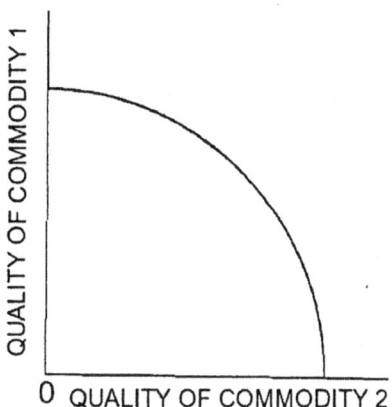

   Which of the following BEST explains the shape of the production possibilities curve for the two-commodity economy shown above? The

   A. opportunity cost of producing an additional unit of each commodity stays the same as production of the commodity expands
   B. opportunity cost of producing an additional unit of each commodity decreases as production of the commodity expands
   C. opportunity cost of producing an additional unit of each commodity increases as production of the commodity expands
   D. quantity demanded of each commodity decreases as consumption of the commodity increases
   E. quantity demanded of each commodity increases as the production of the commodity expands

2. In the long run, compared with a perfectly competitive firm, a monopolistically competitive firm with the same costs will have _____ price and _____ output.

   A. a higher; higher B. a higher; lower
   C. a lower; higher   D. a lower; lower
   E. the same; lower

3. Assume that products X and Y are substitutes.
   If the cost of producing X decreases and the price of Y increases, which of the following will occur to the equilibrium price and quantity of X?

	Price of X	Quantity of X
A.	Increase	Increase
B.	Increase	Decrease
C.	Increase	Increase or decrease
D.	Increase or decrease	Increase
E.	Decrease	Decrease

4. Suppose that an effective minimum wage is imposed in a certain labor market above the equilibrium wage.
   If labor supply in that market subsequently increases, which of the following will occur?

   A. Unemployment in that market will increase.
   B. Quantity of labor supplied will decrease.
   C. Quantity of labor demanded will increase.
   D. Market demand will increase.
   E. The market wage will increase.

5. Imperfectly competitive firms may be allocatively inefficient because they produce at a level of output such that

   A. average cost is at a minimum
   B. price equals marginal revenue
   C. marginal revenue is greater than marginal cost
   D. price equals marginal cost
   E. price is greater than marginal cost

Questions 6-8.

DIRECTIONS: Questions 6 through 8 are to be answered on the basis of the table below, which shows a firm's total cost for different levels of output.

Output	Total Cost
0	$24
1	33
2	41
3	48
4	54
5	61
6	69

6. Which of the following is the firm's marginal cost of producing the fourth unit of output?

   A. $54.00   B. $13.50   C. $7.50   D. $6.00   E. $1.50

7. Which of the following is the firm's average total cost of producing 3 units of output?

   A. $48.00   B. $16.00   C. $14.00   D. $13.50   E. $7.00

8. Which of the following is the firm's average fixed cost of producing 2 units of output?

   A. $24.00   B. $20.50   C. $12.00   D. D, $8.00   E. $7.50

9. In the short run, if the product price of a perfectly competitive firm is less than the minimum average variable cost, the firm will

   A. raise its price
   B. increase its output
   C. decrease its output slightly but increase its profit margin
   D. lose more by continuing to produce than by shutting down
   E. lose less by continuing to produce than by shutting down

10. Which of the following statements is TRUE of perfectly competitive firms in long-run equilibrium?

    A. Firm revenues will decrease if production is increased.
    B. Total firm revenues are at a maximum.
    C. Average fixed cost equals marginal cost.
    D. Average total cost is at a minimum.
    E. Average variable cost is greater than marginal cost.

11. Assume that both input and product markets are competitive. If the product price rises, in the short run firms will increase production by increasing

    A. the stock of fixed capital until marginal revenue equals the product price
    B. the stock of fixed capital until the average product of capital equals the price of capital
    C. labor input until the marginal revenue product of labor equals the wage rate
    D. labor input until the marginal product of labor equals the wage rate
    E. labor input until the ratio of product price to the marginal product of labor equals the wage rate

12. Half of the inhabitants of an island oppose building a new bridge to the mainland, since they say it will destroy the island's quaint atmosphere.
    The economic concept that is MOST relevant to the decision of whether or not to build the bridge is

    A. externalities
    B. natural monopoly
    C. economic rent
    D. imperfect competition
    E. perfect competition

13. Which of the following BEST states the thesis of the law of comparative advantage?

    A. Differences in relative costs of production are the key to determining patterns of trade.
    B. Differences in absolute costs of production determine which goods should be traded between nations.
    C. Tariffs and quotas are beneficial in increasing international competitiveness.
    D. Nations should not specialize in the production of goods and services.
    E. Two nations will not trade if one is more efficient than the other in the production of all goods.

14. A student who attends college would pay $10,000 annually for tuition, books, and fees. If the student's next best alternative is to work and earn $15,000 a year, the opportunity cost of a year in college would be equal to

    A. zero, since the lost opportunity to earn income is offset by the opportunity to attend college
    B. $5,000, representing the difference between forgone income and college costs
    C. $10,000, since opportunity costs include only actual cash outlays
    D. $15,000, representing forgone income, since the costs of tuition, books, and fees will be more than offset by additional income earned after graduation
    E. $25,000, representing the sum of tuition, books, fees, and forgone income

15. If an increase in the price of good X causes a drop in demand for good Y, good Y is a (n)   15.____

    A. inferior good
    B. luxury good
    C. necessary good
    D. substitute for good X
    E. complement to good X

16. An improvement in production technology for a certain good leads to a (n) _____ the good.   16.____

    A. increase in demand for
    B. increase in the supply of
    C. increase in the price of
    D. shortage of
    E. surplus of

17. A firm doubles all of its inputs and finds that it has more than doubled its output. This situation is an example of   17.____

    A. increasing marginal returns
    B. diminishing marginal returns
    C. constant returns to scale
    D. increasing returns to scale
    E. decreasing returns to scale

18. Reducing the tariff on Canadian beer sold in the United States will MOST likely have which of the following effects on the market for beer produced and sold in the United States?   18.____

    A. The quantity of United States beer purchased will increase.
    B. Total expenditure on United States beer will increase.
    C. The supply of United States beer will increase.
    D. The price of United States beer will decrease.
    E. More workers will be employed in the production of United States beer.

19. Suppose that the license paid by each business to operate in a city increases from $400 per year to $500 per year.   19.____
    What effect will this increase have on a firm's short-run costs?

	Marginal Cost	Average Total Cost	Average Variable Cost
A.	Increase	Increase	Increase
B.	Increase	Increase	No effect
C.	No effect	No effect	No effect
D.	No effect	Increase	Increase
E.	No effect	Increase	No effect

20. In a perfectly competitive market, an individual farmer intending to increase her revenue decides to increase the price of her crop by 20 percent.   20.____
    As a result, her total revenue will

    A. decrease
    B. stay the same
    C. increase by less than 20 percent
    D. increase by 20 percent
    E. increase by more than 20 percent

21. If the supply of a factor of production is fixed, which of the following will be TRUE of its price?

   A. Supply is irrelevant to the determination of factor price.
   B. A positive factor price cannot be justified on economic grounds.
   C. Factor price will be determined by the demand for the fixed amount of the factor.
   D. Factor price will not be determined by supply and demand analysis.
   E. Factor price will be zero, since no payment is necessary to secure the services of the factor.

22. Which of the following is TRUE if a perfectly competitive industry is earning zero economic profits in the long run?

   A. The level of investment in long-run equilibrium is greater than the efficient level.
   B. Relatively few firms are able to survive the competitive pressures in the long run.
   C. Some firms will be forced to transfer their resources to more lucrative uses.
   D. The resources invested in this industry are earning at least as high a return as they would in any alternative use.
   E. Firms will exit until economic profits become positive.

23.

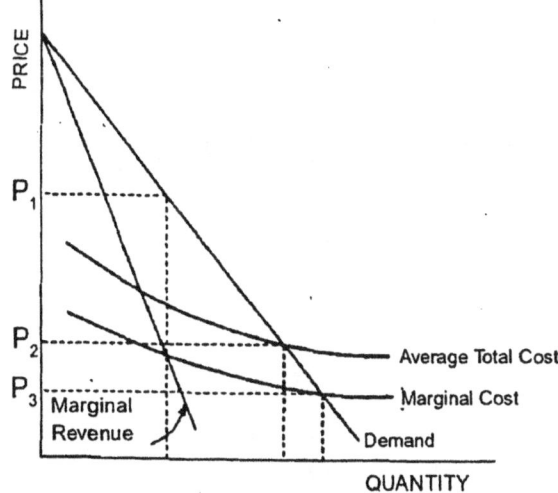

The figure above shows cost and revenue curves for a public regulated power company and three possible prices for its output.
Which of the following statements about those prices Is MOST accurate?

   A. If P_1 were approved, regulation would not be needed and the company would have every incentive to lower rates to P_2.
   B. P_1 is inefficient; it is better to have several utilities serve the area than to approve P_1.
   C. P_2 is ideal; it gives stockholders the maximum rate of return and protects consumers from exploitation.
   D. P_3 would maximize consumer welfare; greater electric use at this low rate would guarantee stockholders a fair rate of return.
   E. P_3 would maximize consumer welfare, but a public subsidy would be needed to keep the company in business.

24. If a competitive firm is faced with an increase in the ad valorem sales tax on its product, it is MOST likely to _____ the entire increase _____ if the elasticity of demand is _____.

    A. shift; to the consumer; infinite
    B. shift; to the consumer; zero
    C. bear; itself; zero
    D. bear; itself; one
    E. shift; to the consumer; one

25. In a market economy, public goods such as community police protection are unlikely to be provided in sufficient quantity by the private sector because

    A. private firms are less efficient at producing public goods than is the government
    B. the use of public goods cannot be withheld from those who do not pay for them
    C. consumers lack information about the benefits of public goods
    D. consumers do not value public goods highly enough for firms to produce them profitably
    E. public goods are inherently too important to be left to private firms to produce

KEY (CORRECT ANSWERS)

1. C		11. C	
2. B		12. A	
3. D		13. A	
4. A		14. E	
5. E		15. E	
6. D		16. B	
7. B		17. D	
8. C		18. D	
9. D		19. E	
10. D		20. A	

21. C
22. D
23. E
24. A
25. B

TEST 2

DIRECTIONS: Each question or incomplete statement is followed by several suggested answers or completions. Select the one that BEST answers the question or completes the statement. *PRINT THE LETTER OF THE CORRECT ANSWER IN THE SPACE AT THE RIGHT.*

1. Problems faced by all economic systems include which of the following? How to
    I. allocate scarce resources among unlimited wants
    II. decentralize markets
    III. decide what to produce, how to produce, and for whom to produce
    IV. set government production quotas
   The CORRECT answer is:

   A. I *only*
   B. I, III
   C. II, III
   D. I, II, III
   E. I, II, III, IV

   1.____

2. Of the following, a fall in the price of a product would be caused by a(n)

   A. increase in population and a decrease in the price of an input
   B. increase in population and a decrease in the number of firms producing the product
   C. increase in average income and an improvement in production technology
   D. decrease in the price of a substitute product and an improvement in production technology
   E. decrease in the price of a substitute product and an increase in the price of an input

   2.____

3. The market equilibrium price of home heating oil is $1.50 per gallon. If a price ceiling of $1.00 per gallon is imposed, which of the following will occur in the market for home heating oil? Quantity
    I. supplied will increase
    II. demanded will increase
    III. supplied will decrease
    IV. demanded will decrease
   The CORRECT answer is:

   A. II *only*
   B. I, II
   C. I, IV
   D. II, III
   E. III, IV

   3.____

4. Suppose that a family buys all its clothing from a discount store and treats these items as inferior goods. Under such circumstances, this family's consumption of discount store clothing will necessarily

   A. increase when a family member wins the state lottery
   B. increase when a family member gets a raise in pay at work
   C. remain unchanged when its income rises or falls due to events beyond the family's control
   D. decrease when a family member becomes unemployed
   E. decrease when a family member experiences an increase in income

   4.____

5. Which of the following describes what will happen to market price and quantity if firms in a perfectly competitive market form a cartel and act as a profit-maximizing monopoly?

	Price	Quantity
A.	Decrease	Decrease
B.	Decrease	Increase
C.	Increase	Increase
D.	Increase	Decrease
E.	Increase	No change

6.

Quantity Produced	Total Cost
0	$5
1	17
2	28
3	41
4	61
5	91

Barney's Bait Company can sell all the lures it produces at the market price of $14. On the basis of the cost information in the table above, how many lures should the bait company make?

A. 1   B. 2   C. 3   D. 4   E. 5

7. A natural monopoly occurs in an industry if

   A. economies of scale allow at most one firm of efficient size to exist in that market
   B. a single firm has control over a scarce and essential resource
   C. a single firm produces inputs for use by other firms
   D. a single firm has the technology to produce the product sold in that market
   E. above-normal profits persist in the industry

8. The typical firm in a monopolistically competitive industry earns zero profit in long-run equilibrium because

   A. advertising costs make monopolistic competition a high-cost market structure rather than a low-cost market structure
   B. the firms in the industry do not operate at the minimum point on their long-run average cost curves
   C. there are no restrictions on entering or exiting from the industry
   D. the firms in the industry are unable to engage in product differentiation
   E. there are close substitutes for each firm's product

9. Of the following, a shift in the market demand for workers with a certain skill is inevitably caused by a (n) _____ workers.

   A. increase in the demand for goods produced by these
   B. decrease in tax rates on the income of these
   C. increase in the equilibrium wages received by these
   D. increase in the supply of these
   E. federally subsidized program created to train new

10. If hiring an additional worker would increase a firm's total cost by less than it would increase its total revenue, the firm should

    A. not hire the worker
    B. hire the worker
    C. hire the worker only if another worker leaves or is fired
    D. hire the worker only if the worker can raise the firm's productivity
    E. reduce the number of workers employed by the firm

11. If a firm wants to produce a given amount of output at the lowest possible cost, it should use each resource in such a manner that

    A. it uses more of the less expensive resource
    B. it uses more of the resource with the highest marginal product
    C. each resource has just reached the point of diminishing marginal returns
    D. the marginal products of each resource are equal
    E. the marginal products per dollar spent on each resource are equal

12. In which of the following ways does the United States government currently intervene in the working of the market economy?
    It
    I. produces certain goods and services
    II. regulates the private sector to achieve a more efficient allocation of resources
    III. redistributes income through taxation and public expenditures
    The CORRECT answer is:

    A. I only   B. II only   C. III only
    D. II, III   E. I, II, III

13. If it were possible to increase the output of military goods and simultaneously to increase the output of the private sector of an economy, which of the following statements about the economy and its current position relative to its production possibilities curve would be TRUE?
    The economy is _____ and _____ the curve.

    A. inefficient; inside   B. inefficient; on
    C. efficient; on   D. efficient; inside
    E. efficient; outside

14. An effective price floor introduced in the market for rice will result in a (n) _____ in the price of rice and a (n) _____ .

    A. decrease; increase in the quantity of rice sold
    B. decrease; decrease in the quantity of rice sold
    C. decrease; excess demand for rice
    D. increase; excess supply of rice
    E. increase; excess demand for rice

15. Marginal revenue is the change in revenue that results from a one-unit increase in the

    A. variable input   B. variable input price
    C. output level   D. output price
    E. fixed cost

16. A leftward shift in the supply curve of corn would result from a (n)

    A. decrease in the price of corn
    B. decrease in the price of farm machinery
    C. increase in the demand for corn bread
    D. increase in the labor costs of producing corn
    E. increase in consumers' incomes

17.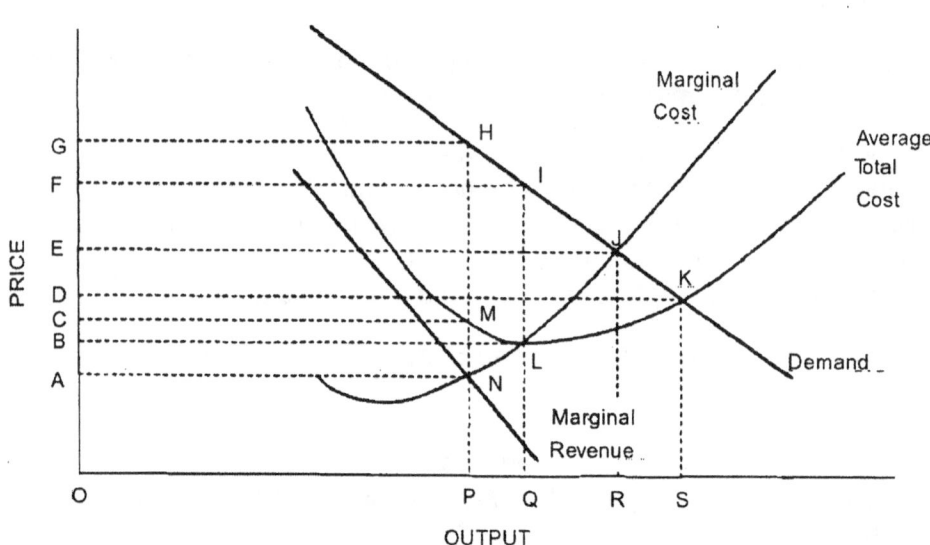

    The diagram above depicts cost and revenue curves for a firm. What are the firm's profit-maximizing output and price?

	Output	Price
A.	OS	OD
B.	OR	OE
C.	OQ	OF
D.	OQ	OB
E.	OP	OG

18. The government is considering imposing a 3 percent tax on either good A or good B. In order to generate the LARGEST revenue, the tax should be imposed on the good for which

    A. demand is perfectly elastic
    B. demand is perfectly inelastic
    C. demand is unit elastic
    D. supply is perfectly elastic
    E. supply is unit elastic

19. Which of the following statements has to be TRUE in a perfectly competitive market?

    A. A firm's marginal revenue equals price.
    B. A firm's average total cost is above price in the long run.
    C. A firm's average fixed cost rises in the short run.
    D. A firm's average variable cost is higher than price in the long run.
    E. Large firms have lower costs than small firms.

20. Assume that an electric power company owns two plants and that, on a particular day, 10,000 kilowatts of electricity are demanded by the public.
    In order to MINIMIZE the total cost of providing the 10,000 kilowatts, the company should allocate production so that

    A. marginal costs are the same for both plants
    B. average total costs are the same for both plants
    C. total variable costs are the same for both plants
    D. the sum of total variable cost and total fixed cost is the same for both plants
    E. only the plant with the lower average cost is used to produce the 10,000 kilowatts of electricity

    20._____

21. Suppose that the consumption of a certain product results in benefits to others besides the consumers of the product.
    Which of the following statements is MOST likely to be true?

    A. The demand for the product is price inelastic.
    B. A perfectly competitive industry will not produce the optimal quantity of the product.
    C. A perfectly competitive industry will not produce the product.
    D. Optimality requires that consumers of this product be taxed.
    E. Producers of this product earn an economic profit.

    21._____

Questions 22-23.

DIRECTIONS: Questions 22 and 23 are to be answered on the basis of the table below, which lists the total output of workers in Greta's Jacket Shop.

Number of Workers	Total Output
2	12
3	22
4	28
5	32

22. Which of the following is the marginal product of the fourth worker?

    A. 4   B. 5   C. 6   D. 28   E. 112

    22._____

23. Greta already employs 3 workers.
    If the price of jackets is $5 and the wage rate is $25, she should

    A. go out of business altogether
    B. lay off the third worker
    C. keep the third worker but not employ more workers
    D. hire two more workers
    E. hire one more worker

    23._____

24. A city council is deciding what price to set for a trip on the city's commuter train line.
    If the council wants to maximize profits, it will set a price so that

    A. price equals marginal cost
    B. price equals average cost
    C. price equals marginal revenue

    24._____

D. marginal revenue equals marginal cost
E. marginal revenue equals average total cost

25. The demand curve for cars is downward sloping because an increase in the price of cars leads to a (n)   25.____

    A. increased use of other modes of transportation
    B. fall in the expected future price of cars
    C. decrease in the number of cars available for purchase
    D. rise in the prices of gasoline and other oil-based products
    E. change in consumers' tastes in cars

KEY (CORRECT ANSWERS)

1. B   11. E
2. D   12. E
3. D   13. A
4. E   14. D
5. D   15. C

6. C   16. D
7. A   17. E
8. C   18. B
9. A   19. A
10. B   20. A

21. B
22. C
23. E
24. D
25. A

EXAMINATION SECTION
TEST 1

DIRECTIONS: Each question or incomplete statement is followed by several suggested answers or completions. Select the one that BEST answers the question or completes the statement. *PRINT THE LETTER OF THE CORRECT ANSWER IN THE SPACE AT THE RIGHT.*

1. The simple circular flow model shows that

    A. households are on the demand side of both product and resource markets
    B. businesses are on the supply side of both product and resource markets
    C. households are on the supply side of the resource market and on the demand side of the product market
    D. businesses are on the demand side of the product market and on the supply side of the resource market

2. The two basic markets shown by the simple circular flow model are

    A. capital goods and consumer goods
    B. free and controlled
    C. product and resource
    D. household and business
    E. competitive and monopolistic

3. In the resource market

    A. businesses borrow money capital from households
    B. businesses sell services to households
    C. households sell resources to businesses
    D. firms sell raw materials to households

4. Which of the following is a limitation of the simple circular flow model?

    A. Intrabusiness and intrahousehold transactions are ignored.
    B. The economic activities of government are omitted.
    C. The determination of product and resource prices is not explained.
    D. All of the above

5. In the simple circular flow model

    A. households are suppliers of resources
    B. businesses are suppliers of final products
    C. households are demanders of final products
    D. all of the above

Questions 6-9.

DIRECTIONS: Questions 6 through 9 are to be answered on the basis of the following circular flow model of the economy.

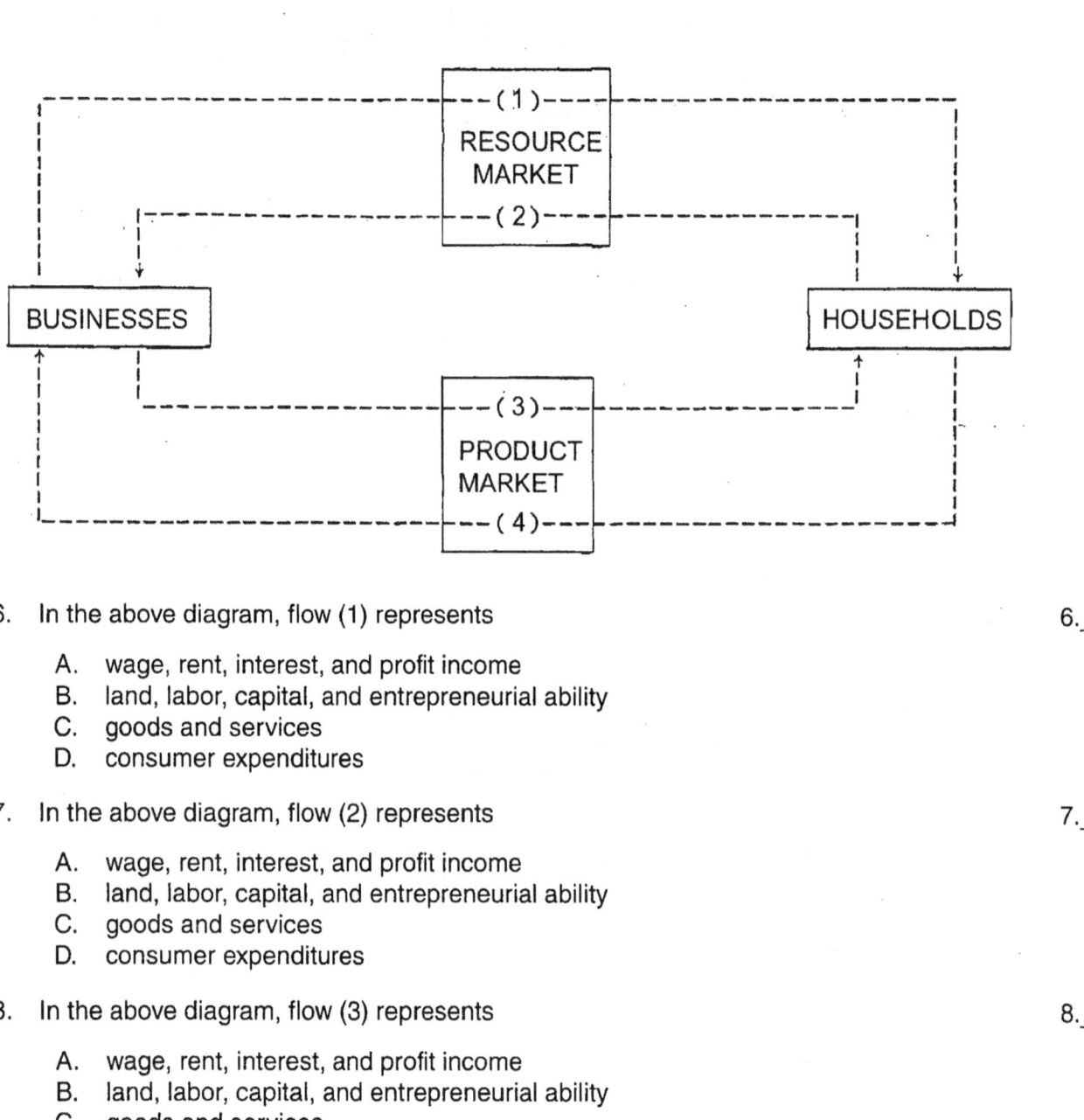

6. In the above diagram, flow (1) represents

   A. wage, rent, interest, and profit income
   B. land, labor, capital, and entrepreneurial ability
   C. goods and services
   D. consumer expenditures

7. In the above diagram, flow (2) represents

   A. wage, rent, interest, and profit income
   B. land, labor, capital, and entrepreneurial ability
   C. goods and services
   D. consumer expenditures

8. In the above diagram, flow (3) represents

   A. wage, rent, interest, and profit income
   B. land, labor, capital, and entrepreneurial ability
   C. goods and services
   D. consumer expenditures

9. In the above diagram, flow (4) represents

   A. wage, rent, interest, and profit income
   B. land, labor, capital, and entrepreneurial ability
   C. goods and services
   D. consumer expenditures

10. In terms of the circular flow diagram, households make expenditures in the _____ market and receive income through the _____ market.

    A. product; financial
    B. resource; product
    C. product; resource
    D. capital; product

11. In terms of the circular flow diagram, businesses obtain revenue through the _____ market and make expenditures in the _____ market.

    A. product; financial
    B. resource; product
    C. product; resource
    D. capital; product

11.____

12. Households and businesses are

    A. both buyers in the resource market
    B. both suppliers in the product market
    C. suppliers in the resource and product markets, respectively
    D. suppliers in the product and resource markets, respectively

12.____

13. In the circular flow model,

    A. households supply resources to firms
    B. households receive income through the resource market
    C. households spend income in the product market
    D. all of the above

13.____

Questions 14-15.

DIRECTIONS: Questions 14 and 15 are to be answered on the basis of the following diagram.

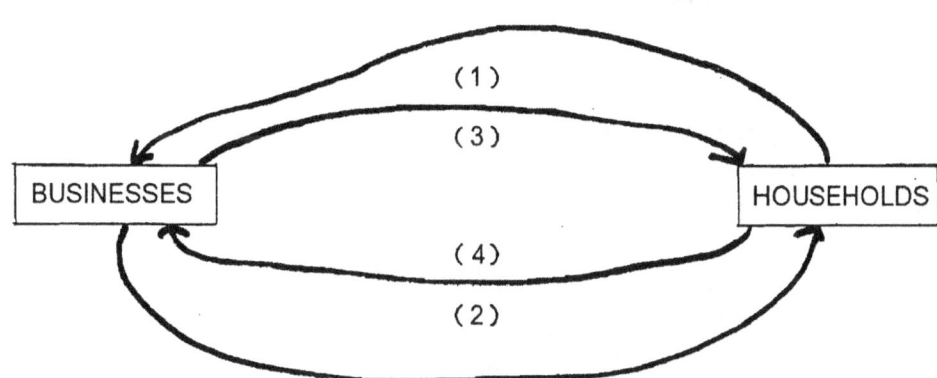

14. In the above diagram, arrows (1) and (2) represent

    A. goods and resources, respectively
    B. money incomes and output, respectively
    C. output and money incomes, respectively
    D. resources and goods, respectively

14.____

15. In the above diagram, arrows (3) and (4) represent

    A. goods and services, respectively
    B. money incomes and consumer expenditures, respectively
    C. resources and goods, respectively
    D. consumer expenditures and money income, respectively

15.____

16. When the price of a product rises, consumers shift their purchases to other products whose prices are now relatively lower.
    This statement describes the

16.____

A. rationing function of prices
B. substitution effect
C. law of supply
D. income effect

17. When the price of a product falls, the purchasing power of our money income rises and thus permits us to purchase more of the product.
This statement describes the

    A. rationing function of prices
    B. substitution effect
    C. law of supply
    D. income effect

17.____

18. During the 1970s, the price of oil rose dramatically, which in turn caused the price of coal to increase. This can best be explained by saying that oil and coal are

    A. complementary goods and the higher price for oil increased the demand for coal
    B. substitute goods and the higher price for oil increased the demand for coal
    C. complementary goods and the higher price for oil decreased the supply of coal
    D. substitute goods and the higher price for oil decreased the supply of coal

18.____

19. An economist for a bicycle company predicts that, other things equal, a rise in consumer incomes will increase the demand for bicycles. This prediction is based upon the assumption that

    A. there are many goods which are substitutes for bicycles
    B. there are many goods which are complementary to bicycles
    C. there are few goods which are substitutes for bicycles
    D. bicycles are normal goods

19.____

20. A rightward shift in the demand curve for product C might be caused by a(n)

    A. increase in income if C is a normal good
    B. decrease in income if C is an inferior good
    C. increase in the price of a product which is a close substitute for C
    D. all of the above

20.____

21. If the price of product L increases, the demand curve for close-substitute product J will

    A. shift downward toward the horizontal axis
    B. shift to the left
    C. shift to the right
    D. remain unchanged

21.____

22. A shift to the right in the demand curve for product A can be most reasonably explained by saying that

    A. consumer incomes have declined and they now want to buy less of A at each possible price
    B. the price of A has increased and, as a result, consumers want to purchase less of it
    C. consumer preferences have changed in favor of A so that they now want to buy more at each possible price

22.____

D. the price of A has declined and, as a result, consumers want to purchase more of it
E. the supply of A has increased because production costs have declined

23. Which of the following will cause the demand curve for product A to shift to the left? 23.____

   A. Population growth which causes an expansion in the number of persons consuming A
   B. An increase in money income if A is a normal good
   C. A decrease in the price of complementary product C
   D. An increase in money income if A is an inferior good
   E. An increase in the price of substitute product B

24. If X is a normal good, a rise in money income will shift the _____ curve for X to the _____. 24.____

   A. supply; left   B. supply; right
   C. demand; left   D. demand; right

25. If Z is an inferior good, a decrease in money income will shift the _____ curve for Z to the _____. 25.____

   A. supply; left   B. supply; right
   C. demand; left   D. demand; right

KEY (CORRECT ANSWERS)

1.	C	11.	C
2.	C	12.	C
3.	C	13.	D
4.	D	14.	D
5.	D	15.	B
6.	A	16.	B
7.	B	17.	D
8.	C	18.	B
9.	D	19.	D
10.	C	20.	D

21. C
22. C
23. D
24. D
25. D

TEST 2

DIRECTIONS: Each question or incomplete statement is followed by several suggested answers or completions. Select the one that BEST answers the question or completes the statement. *PRINT THE LETTER OF THE CORRECT ANSWER IN THE SPACE AT THE RIGHT.*

1. Normal profits are

    A. a cost because any excess of total receipts over total costs will accrue to the businessperson
    B. a cost because they represent payments made for the resources which the businessperson owns and supplies in his or her own enterprise
    C. not a cost because a firm can avoid these payments by temporarily closing down
    D. not a cost of production because they need not be realized in order for a firm to retain entrepreneurial ability

2. Economic profits are

    A. a cost because they are really a part of wage costs
    B. a cost because they accrue to the entrepreneur
    C. not a cost because they cannot be calculated
    D. not an economic cost because they need not be realized in order for a business to acquire and retain entrepreneurial ability

3. If competitive industry Z is realizing substantial economic profits, we can expect that output will

    A. fall, product price will fall, and economic profits will tend to disappear
    B. fall, product price will rise, and economic profits will tend to disappear
    C. expand, product price will fall, and economic profits will tend to disappear
    D. expand, product price will fall, and economic profits will tend to rise

4. When a competitive industry is in equilibrium,

    A. economic profits will be zero
    B. product demand and derived demand are equal
    C. the economizing problem will have been solved for that industry
    D. normal profits will not be realized

5. From society's point of view, the economic function of profits and losses is to

    A. promote the equal distribution of real assets and wealth
    B. perpetuate full employment and price level stability
    C. contribute to a more equal distribution of income
    D. reallocate resources from less desired to more desired uses

6. In 1994 Ford sold 500,000 Escorts at an average price of $7,200 per car; in 1995, 600,000 Escorts were sold at an average price of $7,500 per car. These statements

A. suggest that the demand for Escorts decreased between 1994 and 1995
B. imply that Escorts are an inferior good
C. suggest that the demand for Escorts increased between 1994 and 1995
D. illustrate that the supply curve for Escorts is down-sloping

7. Other things equal, which of the following might shift the demand curve for gasoline to the left?

    A. The discovery of vast new oil reserves in Montana
    B. The development of a low-cost electric automobile
    C. An increase in the price of train and air transportation
    D. A large decline in the price of automobiles

8. A decrease in the price of cameras will

    A. cause the demand curve for film to become vertical
    B. shift the demand curve for film to the right
    C. shift the demand curve for film to the left
    D. not affect the demand for film

9. If products C and D are close substitutes, an increase in the price of C will shift the demand curve of

    A. C to the left and the demand curve of D to the right
    B. D to the right
    C. both products to the right
    D. both products to the left

10. In constructing a stable demand curve for product X,

    A. consumer preferences are assumed constant
    B. the prices of other goods are assumed given
    C. money incomes are assumed constant
    D. all of the above assumptions are made

11. The demand curve for a product might shift as the result of a change in

    A. consumer incomes
    B. the prices of related goods
    C. the number of buyers in the market
    D. all of the above

12. Suppose an excise tax is imposed on product X. We would expect this tax to

    A. increase the demand for complementary good Y and decrease the demand for substitute product Z
    B. decrease the demand for complementary good Y and increase the demand for substitute product Z
    C. increase the demands for both complementary good Y and substitute product Z
    D. decrease the demands for both complementary good Y and substitute product Z

13. When an economist says that the demand for a product has increased, this means that

    A. consumers are now willing to purchase more of this product at each possible price
    B. the product has become particularly scarce for some reason
    C. product price has fallen and as a consequence consumers are buying a larger quantity of the product
    D. the demand curve has shifted to the left

14. The term *quantity demanded* refers to

    A. the entire series of prices and quantities which comprise the demand schedule
    B. a situation where the income and substitution effects do not apply
    C. the amount of a product which will be purchased at some specific price
    D. none of the above

15. Assume that the demand schedule for product C is down-sloping. If the price of C falls from $2.00 to $1.75,

    A. a smaller quantity of C will be demanded
    B. a larger quantity of C will be demanded
    C. the demand for C will increase
    D. the demand for C will decrease

16. The law of supply

    A. reflects the amounts which producers will want to offer at each price in a series of prices
    B. is reflected in an upsloping supply curve
    C. shows that the relationship between price and quantity supplied is positive
    D. is reflected in all of the above

17. A firm"s supply curve is upsloping because

    A. the expansion of production necessitates the use of qualitatively inferior inputs
    B. mass production economies are associated with larger levels of output
    C. consumers envision a positive relationship between price and quality
    D. beyond some point the production costs of additional units of output will rise

18. A leftward shift of a product supply curve might be caused by

    A. an improvement in the relevant technique of production
    B. a decline in the prices of needed inputs
    C. an increase in consumer incomes
    D. some firms leaving an industry

19. The location of the product supply curve depends upon

    A. production technology
    B. the number of sellers in the market
    C. costs of required resources
    D. all of the above

20. An improvement in production technology will   20.____

    A. tend to increase equilibrium price
    B. shift the supply curve to the left
    C. shift the supply curve to the right
    D. shift the demand curve to the left

21. Because of unseasonably cold weather, the supply of oranges has substantially   21.____
    decreased.
    This statement indicates that

    A. consumers will be willing and able to buy fewer oranges at each possible price
    B. the demand for oranges will necessarily rise
    C. the equilibrium quantity of oranges will rise
    D. the amount of oranges that will be available at various prices has declined
    E. the price of oranges will fall

22. If producers must obtain higher prices than previously in order to produce various levels   22.____
    of output, one can say that there has occurred a (n)

    A. decrease in demand   B. increase in demand
    C. decrease in supply   D. increase in supply

23. Other things the same, we can expect the imposition of an excise tax on a product to   23.____

    A. decrease its supply
    B. increase its price
    C. decrease the quantity sold
    D. all of the above

24. In a market economy, a significant change in the demand for product X will   24.____

    A. alter the profits or losses received by certain firms
    B. cause a reallocation of scarce resources
    C. cause some industries to expand and others to contract
    D. all of the above

25. If competitive industry Y is incurring substantial losses, we can expect that output will   25.____

    A. expand, product price will rise, and losses will tend to disappear
    B. contract, product price will fall, and losses will increase
    C. contract, product price will rise, and losses will tend to disappear
    D. expand, product price will fall, and losses will tend to disappear

KEY (CORRECT ANSWERS)

1. B
2. D
3. C
4. A
5. D

6. C
7. B
8. B
9. B
10. D

11. D
12. B
13. A
14. C
15. B

16. D
17. B
18. D
19. D
20. C

21. D
22. C
23. D
24. D
25. B

TEST 3

DIRECTIONS: Each question or incomplete statement is followed by several suggested answers or completions. Select the one that BEST answers the question or completes the statement. *PRINT THE LETTER OF THE CORRECT ANSWER IN THE SPACE AT THE RIGHT.*

1. If an increase occurs in the demand for product X, we would expect all of the following to occur EXCEPT a(n)

    A. increase in the profits of industry X
    B. increase in the demand for resources employed by industry X
    C. increase in the output of industry X
    D. decrease in the prices of resources employed in industry X

2. The economic function of profits and losses is to

    A. bring about a more equal distribution of income
    B. signal that resources should be reallocated
    C. eliminate small firms and reduce competition
    D. tell government which industries need to be subsidized

3. In a competitive economy, prices influence

    A. consumers in their purchases of goods and services
    B. businesses in their purchases of economic resources
    C. workers in making occupational choices
    D. all of the above

4. If a competitive industry is neither expanding nor contracting, we would expect

    A. normal profits to be zero
    B. economic profits to be zero
    C. consumer demand and derived demand to be equal
    D. external costs or benefits to be large

5. Suppose a firm's total economic cost in producing 1,000 aluminum baseball bats is $10,000. These bats are then sold by the firm for $12,000. We can conclude that

    A. the firm is necessarily using the least-cost production technique because it is realizing an economic profit
    B. the firm's normal profit is $2,000
    C. the firm's pure or economic profit is $2,000
    D. there is no economic reason for the aluminum bat industry to either expand or contract

6. Suppose industry A is realizing substantial economic profits. Which of the following best describes the adjustment process which would bring about a new equilibrium?
   Firms will _____ the industry, output will _____, and product price will _____.

    A. leave; fall; rise   B. enter; rise; rise
    C. leave; rise; fall   D. enter; rise; fall

7. An industry is in equilibrium when

   A. normal profits are zero
   B. total revenue exceeds total economic costs
   C. total economic costs exceed total revenue
   D. economic profits are zero

8. When economists say that the demand for a resource is a *derived demand,* they mean that

   A. producers tend to substitute low-priced for high-priced resources
   B. the demand for resources depends upon the demand for the product which those resources produce
   C. government demand complements private demand for most goods and services
   D. resource demand curves are often upsloping

9. The competitive market system

   A. encourages innovation because government provides tax breaks and subsidies to those who develop new products or new productive techniques
   B. discourages innovation because it is difficult to acquire additional capital in the form of new machinery and equipment
   C. discourages innovation because firms want to get all the profits possible from existing machinery and equipment
   D. encourages innovation because successful innovators are rewarded with economic profits

10. The most efficient combination of resources in producing any output is that combination which

    A. comes closest to using the same quantities of land, labor, capital, and entrepreneurial ability
    B. can be obtained for the smallest money outlay
    C. uses the smallest total quantity of all resources
    D. conserves most on the use of labor

Questions 11-14.

DIRECTIONS: Questions 11 through 14 are to be answered on the basis of the following data which show all available techniques by which 20 units of a given commodity can be produced.

Resource	Resource Prices	Possible Production Techniques				
		#1	#2	#3	#4	#5
Land	$4	2	4	2	4	4
Labor	3	1	2	4	1	3
Capital	3	5	2	3	1	2
Entrepreneurial ability	2	3	1	1	4	1

11. Given the indicated resource prices, the economically most efficient production technique(s) will be technique(s)

    A. #1   B. #2 and #4   C. #3
    D. #1 and #3   E. #5

12. Assuming that the firm is motivated by self-interest and that the 20 units which can be produced with each technique can be sold for $2 per unit, the firm will

   A. realize an economic profit of $10
   B. realize an economic profit of $4
   C. only make a normal profit
   D. just manage to cover all of its costs
   E. close down rather than incur a loss by producing

12._____

13. Which of the following statements concerning this industry is CORRECT?

   A. Firms in this industry will find that firms in other industries are able to outbid them for resources.
   B. The industry will contract as firms are forced out of business.
   C. The industry will expand as new firms enter.
   D. The industry is in equilibrium in that there is no reason for it to expand or contract.

13._____

14. If a new production technique is developed which enables a firm to produce 20 units of output with 3 units of land, 3 of labor, 1 of capital, and 2 of entrepreneurial ability, this technique would

   A. not be adopted because although it reduces production costs, it does not increase profits
   B. be adopted because it would lower production costs and increase economic profits
   C. not be adopted because it entails higher production costs than other available techniques
   D. be adopted, even though economic profits would be reduced slightly

14._____

Questions 15-16.

DIRECTIONS: Questions 15 and 16 are to be answered on the basis of the following information: Suppose 30 units of product A can be produced by employing just labor and capital in the four ways shown below. Assume the prices of labor and capital are $2 and $3, respectively.

	Production Techniques			
	I	II	III	IV
Labor	4	3	2	5
Capital	2	3	5	1

15. Which technique is economically most efficient in producing A?

   A. I B. II C. III D. IV

15._____

16. If the price of product A is $.50, the firm will realize a (n)

   A. economic profit of $4
   B. economic profit of $2
   C. economic profit of $6
   D. loss of $3

16._____

17. In a competitive market economy, firms will select the least-cost production technique because

17._____

A. such choices will result in the full employment of available resources
B. to do so will maximize firm profits
C. this will prevent new firms from entering the industry
D. *dollar voting* by consumers mandates such a choice

18. The *invisible hand* refers to the

    A. fact that our tax system redistributes income from rich to poor
    B. notion that, under competition, decisions motivated by self-interest promote the social interest
    C. tendency of monopolistic sellers to raise prices above competitive levels
    D. fact that government controls the functioning of the market system

19. Two major virtues of the competitive market system are that it

    A. allocates resources efficiently and allows economic freedom
    B. results in an equitable personal distribution of income and always maintains full employment
    C. results in price level stability and a fair personal distribution of income
    D. eliminates discrimination and minimizes environmental pollution

20. Supporters of the market system

    A. contend that it is conducive to the efficient use of scarce resources
    B. argue that it effectively harnesses the incentives of workers and entrepreneurs
    C. believe it is consistent with freedom of choice
    D. all of the above

21. The price elasticity of demand coefficient indicates

    A. buyer responsiveness to price changes
    B. the extent to which a demand curve shifts as incomes change
    C. the slope of the demand curve
    D. how far business executives can stretch their fixed costs

22. The basic formula for the price elasticity of demand coefficient is

    A. absolute decline in quantity demanded/absolute increase in price
    B. percentage change in quantity demanded/percentage change in price
    C. absolute decline in price/absolute increase in quantity demanded
    D. percentage change in price/percentage change in quantity demanded

23. The demand for a product is said to be inelastic with respect to price if

    A. consumers are largely unresponsive to a per unit price change
    B. the elasticity coefficient is greater than 1
    C. a drop in price is accompanied by a decrease in the quantity demanded
    D. a drop in price is accompanied by an increase in the quantity demanded

24. If the price elasticity of demand for a product is 2.5, then a price cut from $2.00 to $1.80 will _____ the quantity demanded by about _____ percent.

    A. increase; 2.5　　　　　　　B. decrease; 2.5
    C. increase; 25　　　　　　　　D. increase; 250

25. Suppose that as the price of Y falls from $2.00 to $1.90, the quantity of Y demanded increases from 110 to 118.
It can be concluded that the price elasticity of demand is

    A. 4.00   B. 2.09   C. 1.37   D. 3.94

25.____

KEY (CORRECT ANSWERS)

1. D		11. B	
2. B		12. A	
3. D		13. C	
4. B		14. B	
5. C		15. D	
6. D		16. B	
7. D		17. B	
8. B		18. B	
9. D		19. A	
10. B		20. D	

21. A
22. B
23. A
24. C
25. C

TEST 4

DIRECTIONS: Each question or incomplete statement is followed by several suggested answers or completions. Select the one that BEST answers the question or completes the statement. *PRINT THE LETTER OF THE CORRECT ANSWER IN THE SPACE AT THE RIGHT.*

1. If the demand for product X is inelastic, a 4 percent increase in the price of X will _____ the quantity of X demanded by _____ than 4 percent.

    A. decrease; more
    B. decrease; less
    C. increase; more
    D. increase; less

    1.____

2. A perfectly inelastic demand schedule

    A. rises upward and to the right, but has a constant slope
    B. can be represented by a line parallel to the vertical axis
    C. cannot be shown on a two-dimensional graph
    D. can be represented by a line parallel to the horizontal axis

    2.____

3. A given leftward shift in the supply curve of product X will increase equilibrium price to a greater extent the

    A. more elastic the supply curve
    B. larger the elasticity of demand coefficient
    C. more elastic the demand for the product
    D. more inelastic the demand for the product

    3.____

4. The price of product X is reduced from $100 to $90 and, as a result, the quantity demanded increases from 50 to 60 units. From this we can conclude that the demand for X in this price range

    A. has declined
    B. is of unit elasticity
    C. is inelastic
    D. is elastic

    4.____

5. The diagram shown at the right shows two product demand curves. On the basis of this diagram, we can say that

    A. over range $P_1 P_2$ price elasticity of demand is greater for D_1 than for D_2
    B. over range $P_1 P_2$ price elasticity of demand is greater for D_2 than for D_1
    C. over range $P_1 P_2$ price elasticity is the same for the two demand curves
    D. not enough information is given to compare price elasticities

    5.____

68

6. The concept of price elasticity of demand measures the

   A. slope of the demand curve
   B. number of buyers in a market
   C. extent to which the demand curve shifts as the result of a price decline
   D. sensitivity of consumers to price changes

7. If the price elasticity of demand for gasoline is 0.20, this indicates that

   A. the demand for gasoline is linear
   B. a rise in the price of gasoline will reduce the total revenue going to sellers
   C. a 10 percent rise in the price of gasoline will decrease the amount purchased by 2 percent
   D. a 10 percent fall in the price of gasoline will increase the amount purchased by 20 percent

8. The demands for such products as salt, bread, and electricity tend to be

   A. perfectly price inelastic
   B. perfectly price elastic
   C. relatively price inelastic
   D. relatively price elastic

9. The demand for mass transit by commuters is likely to be

   A. more price elastic in the short run than in the long run
   B. more price elastic in the long run than in the short run
   C. of unitary elasticity
   D. nearly perfectly inelastic because there are no close substitutes

10. The demand for beer is likely to be

    A. less elastic than the demand for Budweiser
    B. more elastic than the demand for Budweiser
    C. of the same elasticity as the demand for Budweiser
    D. perfectly inelastic

11. An antidrug policy which reduces the supply of heroin will tend to _____ street crime because the addict's demand for heroin is highly _____.

    A. increase; inelastic   B. reduce; elastic
    C. reduce; inelastic   D. increase; elastic

12. Other things the same, the shortage associated with a price ceiling will be greater the

    A. smaller the elasticity of both demand and supply
    B. greater the elasticity of both demand and supply
    C. greater the elasticity of supply and the smaller the elasticity of demand
    D. greater the elasticity of demand and the smaller the elasticity of supply

13. Price ceilings and price floors

    A. cause surpluses and shortages, respectively
    B. make the rationing function of free markets more efficient
    C. interfere with the rationing function of prices
    D. shift demand and supply curves and, therefore, have no effect upon the rationing function of prices

14. Students at Twin Peaks State University pay $40 per year for a parking permit but many complain that they are unable to find a parking place in University lots. This suggests that

    A. student incomes are too low
    B. parking permits are underpriced
    C. parking permits are overpriced
    D. the University should make parking free

15. An effective minimum wage law can be expected to

    A. clear the market for blue-collar workers
    B. increase the number of firms in those industries wherein the law is effective
    C. increase employment for some affected workers
    D. cause unemployment for some affected workers

16. At the current price, there is a shortage of a product. We would expect price to _____, quantity demanded to _____, and quantity supplied to _____.

    A. decrease; decrease; increase
    B. decrease; decrease; decrease
    C. decrease; increase; decrease
    D. increase; decrease; increase

17. A surplus of a product will arise when price is _____ equilibrium with the result that quantity _____ exceeds quantity _____.

    A. above; demanded; supplied
    B. above; supplied; demanded
    C. below; demanded; supplied
    D. below; supplied; demanded

18. If we say that a price is *too high to clear the market,* we mean that

    A. quantity demanded exceeds quantity supplied
    B. the equilibrium price is above the current price
    C. quantity supplied exceeds quantity demanded
    D. the price of the good is likely to rise

19. Assume in a competitive market that price is initially above the equilibrium level. We can predict that price will _____, quantity demanded will _____, and quantity supplied will _____.

    A. decrease; decrease; increase
    B. decrease; decrease; decrease

C. decrease; increase; decrease
D. increase; decrease; increase

20. Assume in a competitive market that price is initially below the equilibrium level. We can predict that price will _____, quantity demanded will _____, and quantity supplied will _____.

    A. decrease; decrease; increase
    B. decrease; decrease; decrease
    C. decrease; increase; decrease
    D. increase; decrease; increase

21. In which of the following instances will the effect upon equilibrium price be indeterminant, that is, dependent upon the magnitude of the given shifts in supply and demand?

    A. Demand rises and supply rises.
    B. Supply falls and demand remains constant.
    C. Demand rises and supply falls.
    D. Supply rises and demand falls.

22. An unusually bountiful crop of coffee beans might be expected to

    A. increase the supply of coffee
    B. reduce the price of coffee
    C. increase the quantity of coffee consumed
    D. lower the price of tea

23. Data from the registrar's office at Michigan State University indicate that over the past twenty years tuition and enrollment have both increased. From this information we can conclude that

    A. higher education is an exception to the law of demand
    B. the supply of education provided by MSU has also increased over the twenty-year period
    C. school-age population, incomes, and preferences for education have changed over the twenty-year period
    D. MSU's supply curve of education is downsloping

24. The rationing function of prices refers to the

    A. tendency of supply and demand to shift in opposite directions
    B. fact that ration coupons are needed to alleviate wartime shortages of goods
    C. capacity of a competitive market to equate the quantity demanded and the quantity supplied
    D. ability of the market system to generate an equitable distribution of income

25. Depreciation of the dollar will tend to

    A. decrease the prices of both American imports and exports
    B. increase the prices of both American imports and exports
    C. decrease the prices of the goods Americans import, but increase the prices to foreigners of the goods Americans export
    D. increase the prices of the goods Americans import, but decrease the prices to foreigners of the goods Americans export

KEY (CORRECT ANSWERS)

1.	B	11.	A
2.	B	12.	B
3.	D	13.	C
4.	B	14.	B
5.	D	15.	C
6.	D	16.	B
7.	C	17.	B
8.	C	18.	C
9.	B	19.	C
10.	A	20.	D

21. A
22. A
23. C
24. C
25. D

EXAMINATION SECTION
TEST 1

DIRECTIONS: Each question or incomplete statement is followed by several suggested answers or completions. Select the one that BEST answers the question or completes the statement. *PRINT THE LETTER OF THE CORRECT ANSWER IN THE SPACE AT THE RIGHT.*

1. The addition of government to the circular flow model illustrates that government may affect the

    A. level of resource use
    B. allocation of resources
    C. distribution of income
    D. all of the above

    1.____

2. The economic policies and programs of government can affect the

    A. distribution of income
    B. allocation of resources
    C. level of domestic output
    D. all of the above

    2.____

3. Government may lessen income inequality by

    A. providing transfer payments to the poor
    B. directly modifying market prices as, for example, by establishing a legal minimum wage
    C. using the tax system to tax the wealthy relatively more heavily than the poor
    D. all of the above

    3.____

4. External costs arise

    A. when firms pay more than the opportunity cost of resources
    B. when the demand curve for a product is located too far to the left
    C. when firms use resources without being compelled to pay for them
    D. only in capitalistic societies

    4.____

5. External benefits refer to

    A. benefits which accrue to parties other than the producer and buyer of a good
    B. the benefits which resource suppliers obtain from the production and sale of a good
    C. the benefit which a consumer receives from buying a good
    D. the combined benefits which buyer and seller receive from a voluntary market transaction

    5.____

6. If there are important spillover benefits associated with the consumption of a product, it can be said that

    A. government should enact legislation to prohibit the production of the commodity
    B. special excise taxes should be levied on producers of the product
    C. the market demand curve understates the relative importance of the product and resources are therefore underallocated to its production
    D. the market supply curve for the product lies too far to the right to provide an efficient allocation of resources

    6.____

73

7. Suppose a product entails substantial spillover costs. If government adopts a policy which forces producers to pay these costs, the

   A. output of the product will decrease
   B. initial misallocation of resources will be intensified
   C. output of the product will increase
   D. price of the product will decrease

8. Suppose it is determined that people with more education are less likely to be unemployed and less likely to receive government welfare payments. This suggests that education

   A. is not subject to the exclusion principle
   B. entails external benefits
   C. entails a free-rider problem
   D. should be produced in the private sector

9. A public good can be best defined as one which

   A. has no spillovers associated with its production or consumption
   B. entails rising costs of production
   C. yields widespread benefits which cannot readily be denied the public at large
   D. yields benefits only to the individual who decides to buy it

10. The market system fails to produce public goods because

    A. there is no need or demand for such goods
    B. private firms cannot restrict the benefits of such goods to consumers who are willing to pay for them
    C. public enterprises can produce such goods at lower cost than can private enterprises
    D. their production seriously distorts the distribution of income

11. The exclusion principle is the notion that

    A. those who are unable or unwilling to pay the market price for a good are excluded from the benefits which that product provides
    B. cases of market failure cannot be remedied by government actions
    C. the presence of external costs and benefits result in misallocations of resources
    D. people can receive benefits from goods without contributing to their production costs

12. The production of economically desirable public goods must be sponsored by government because

    A. the existence of large spillover costs precludes their production in the private sector
    B. public goods have characteristics which make it difficult or impossible for private firms to produce them profitably
    C. the benefits derived from their production exceed the costs of producing them
    D. the law of increasing marginal opportunity costs does not apply to public goods

13. An example of a public good is 13.____

    A. a movie theater
    B. a freight train
    C. a lighthouse
    D. Disneyland

14. Private firms will not provide such goods as lighthouses or flood-control projects because 14.____

    A. such projects generate harmful spillover effects
    B. marginal benefits invariably fall short of marginal costs in such projects
    C. these are major sources of revenue for government
    D. there is no way of denying benefits to those who are unwilling to pay

15. The *free-rider problem* refers to the fact that 15.____

    A. government subsidizes the fares of many municipal mass-transit systems
    B. government arbitrarily attaches excise taxes to a select list of goods and services
    C. the benefits associated with public goods cannot be denied to those who are unwilling to pay for them
    D. some people receive income from welfare programs to which they are not entitled

Questions 16-18.

DIRECTIONS: Questions 16 through 18 are to be answered on the basis of the following diagram.

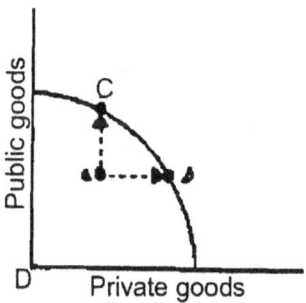

16. The movement from point b to point c suggests that more 16.____

    A. private goods are being produced at the expense of fewer public goods
    B. public goods are being produced at the expense of fewer private goods
    C. public goods are being produced by employing currently idle resources
    D. private goods are being produced by employing currently idle resources

17. The movement from point a to point c suggests that more 17.____

    A. private goods are being produced by employing currently idle resources
    B. public goods are being produced by employing currently idle resources
    C. public goods are being produced at the expense of fewer private goods
    D. private goods are being produced at the expense of fewer public goods

18. The movement from point b to point c can be achieved by _____ taxes and _____ government spending. 18.____

    A. increasing; increasing
    B. increasing; decreasing
    C. decreasing; increasing
    D. decreasing; decreasing

19. The stabilization function of government entails government's efforts to

   A. alter the output of specific goods when external costs or benefits are present
   B. reduce the after-tax incomes of the rich and increase the after-tax incomes of the poor
   C. deal with the problems of substantial unemployment and rapid inflation
   D. provide the socially desired output of public goods

20. A(n) _____ would not be appropriate if government were attempting to restrain a dramatic rise in the general price level.

   A. increase in tax rates
   B. decrease in subsidies to businesses
   C. increase in transfer payments to households
   D. decrease in government spending

21. An increase in _____ would not be appropriate if government were attempting to alleviate a serious recession.

   A. tax rates
   B. subsidies to businesses
   C. transfer payments to households
   D. government spending

Questions 22-24.

DIRECTIONS: Questions 22 through 24 are to be answered on the basis of the following data.

Taxable Income	Total Tax
$1,000	$ 0
2,000	100
3,000	300
4,000	600
5,000	1,000
6,000	1,500

22. The tax represented above is

   A. perverse   B. proportional
   C. regressive   D. progressive

23. If your taxable income is $4,000, your average tax rate will be _____ percent.

   A. 20   B. 17   C. 15   D. 10

24. If your taxable income increases from $4,000 to $5,000, you will encounter a marginal tax rate of _____ percent.

   A. 40   B. 25   C. 15   D. 10

25. In a market for pollution rights, an increase in demand would

   A. raise the price of pollution rights, but leave the quantity unchanged
   B. stimulate the economic incentive to pollute
   C. increase the actual amount of pollution
   D. induce an increase in the supply of pollution rights

26. The creation of markets for pollution rights would provide 26._____

    A. neither an incentive not to pollute nor revenue for environmental improvement
    B. funds for environmental improvement, but would not provide an incentive to refrain from polluting
    C. an incentive not to pollute, but would not provide funds for environmental improvement
    D. both an incentive not to pollute and revenue which could be devoted to environmental improvement

27. The creation of a market for pollution rights would 27._____

    A. reduce air and water pollution to zero
    B. stimulate the search for pollution-reducing technologies
    C. induce an increase in the supply of pollution rights
    D. be in conflict with the concept of user charges

Questions 28-29.

DIRECTIONS: Questions 28 and 29 are to be answered on the basis of the following diagram.

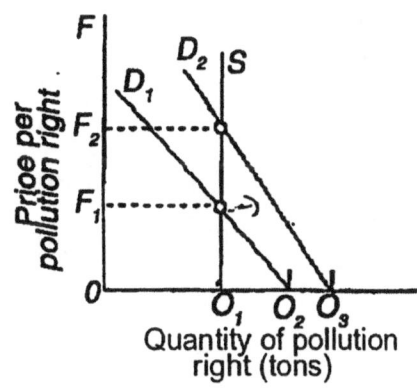

28. Which of the following would best explain the P_1 to P_2 increase in price of pollution rights? 28._____

    A. Implementation of improved technology for reducing pollution
    B. An expansion of the number of firms
    C. A subsidy of P_1P_2 to polluters
    D. A shift of the supply curve of pollution rights from some point to the left of S to S

29. Without this market for pollution rights, the quantity (tons) of pollution would be 29._____

    A. Q_3, if demand is D_2 B. Q_1, if demand is D_1
    C. Q_2, if demand is D_2 D. Q_1, if demand is D_2

30. A monopolistically competitive industry combines elements of both competition and monopoly. The monopoly element results from

    A. the likelihood of collusion
    B. high entry barriers
    C. product differentiation
    D. mutual interdependence in decision making

30.____

KEY (CORRECT ANSWERS)

1.	D	16.	B
2.	D	17.	B
3.	D	18.	A
4.	A	19.	C
5.	A	20.	C
6.	D	21.	A
7.	A	22.	D
8.	B	23.	C
9.	C	24.	A
10.	B	25.	A
11.	A	26.	D
12.	B	27.	B
13.	C	28.	B
14.	D	29.	A
15.	C	30.	C

TEST 2

DIRECTIONS: Each question or incomplete statement is followed by several suggested answers or completions. Select the one that BEST answers the question or completes the statement. *PRINT THE LETTER OF THE CORRECT ANSWER IN THE SPACE AT THE RIGHT.*

1. American exports and imports of goods and services average about _____ percent of GDP. 1.____

    A. 2-3 B. 11-13 C. 25-28 D. 30-32

2. Our most important trading partner quantitatively is 2.____

    A. Mexico B. Canada C. Germany D. Japan

3. The bulk of the United States international trade is with 3.____

    A. the nations of Eastern Europe
    B. the less developed countries of Africa, Asia, and Latin America
    C. other industrialized nations, e.g., Canada, Japan, and the countries of Western Europe
    D. China

4. Multinational corporations 4.____

    A. mainly are headquartered in Switzerland
    B. are so named because of their heavy export volume
    C. are illegal under the United States antitrust laws
    D. are so named because of their sizable foreign production and distribution assets

5. The circular flow model reveals that an increase in American exports will 5.____

    A. reduce revenue to American businesses and increase money income to American resource suppliers
    B. decrease output and money income in the rest of the world, further boosting our imports
    C. increase revenue to American businesses and increase money income to American resource suppliers
    D. increase American imports by more than the increase in exports

6. Other things equal, if incomes decline significantly in Canada, western Europe, and Japan, we would expect 6.____

    A. no significant impact on the American economy
    B. an increase in American exports and a decline in money income flowing to American households
    C. a decline in American exports and a decrease in money income flowing to American households
    D. an increase in the foreign demand for dollars

7. Answer this question on the basis of the following production possibilities data for Gamma and Sigma. All data are in tons.

   Gamma production possibilities:

	A	B	C	D	E
Tea	120	90	60	30	0
Pots	0	30	60	90	120

   Sigma production possibilities:

	A	B	C	D	E
Tea	40	30	20	10	0
Pots	0	30	60	90	120

   Referring to the above data, assume that before specialization and trade Gamma and Sigma both chose production possibility C. Now, if each specializes according to comparative advantage, the gains from specialization and trade will be
   A. 40 tons of pots
   B. 20 tons of tea and 20 tons of pots
   C. 20 tons of tea
   D. 40 tons of tea

8. Answer this question on the basis of the following production possibilities data for two countries, Alpha and Beta, which have populations of equal size.

   Alpha's production possibilities:

	A	B	C	D	E
Fish (tons)	80	60	40	20	0
Chips (tons)	0	5	10	15	20

   Beta's production possibilities:

	A	B	C	D	E
Fish (tons)	240	180	120	60	0
Chips (tons)	0	10	20	30	40

   Referring to the above data, suppose that before specialization and trade Alpha chose production alternative C and Beta chose production alternative B. After specialization and trade, the gains will be
   A. 20 tons of fish
   B. 20 tons of chips
   C. 20 tons of fish and 20 tons of chips
   D. 240 tons of fish and 20 tons of chips

9. *Fast track* means that the President has the power to negotiate trade accords and submit them to Congress for a vote with no

   A. debate
   B. amendments
   C. discussion
   D. cross-party voting

10. A trade bloc is a(n)

    A. tariff or quota which impedes imports
    B. group of nations which allows free trade among member nations but restricts imports from non-member nations via tariffs and quotas
    C. area of a nation where manufacturers can import product components without paying tariffs
    D. group of nations which advertise their common export goods abroad

11. The main problem posed by trade blocs for non-member nations is that

    A. member nations may achieve growth rates which exceed those of non-member nations
    B. non-members must exchange their currencies for foreign monies before they can engage in export or import transactions
    C. non-members face tariffs which member nations do not
    D. member nations refuse to participate in tariff negotiations sponsored by GATT

12. The European Union (EU) comprises a group of European nations which have

    A. abolished tariffs among one another and established
    B. a system of common tariffs with respect to non-member nations
    C. fully integrated their economies by establishing a central bank, a common currency, and a coordinated set of governmental budgetary policies
    D. agreed to trade only among one another
    E. eliminated all tariffs and trade barriers with non-member nations

13. The North American Free Trade Agreement (NAFTA)

    A. resulted from GATT negotiations at the Uruguay Round
    B. established a free trade zone encompassing Canada, Mexico, and the United States
    C. is also known as the Reciprocal Trade Act
    D. permits the former republics of the Soviet Union to export goods duty free to North America

14. Critics of the North American Free Trade Agreement (NAFTA) contend it will

    A. increase the flow of illegal Mexican immigrants to the United States
    B. cause the European Union and Japan to raise trade barriers against American goods
    C. cause the loss of American jobs to Mexico
    D. increase foreign ownership of assets in the United States

15. A market in which the money of one nation is exchanged for the money of another nation is a _____ market.

    A. resource   B. financial
    C. futures   D. foreign exchange

16. American export transactions create a(n)

   A. American demand for foreign monies and the satisfaction of this demand decreases the supplies of dollars held by foreign banks
   B. American demand for foreign monies and the satisfaction of this demand increases the supplies of dollars held by foreign banks
   C. foreign demand for dollars and the satisfaction of this demand decreases the supplies of foreign monies held
   D. by American banks
   E. foreign demand for dollars and the satisfaction of this demand increases the supplies of foreign monies held by American banks

17. American import transactions create a(n)

   A. foreign demand for dollars and the satisfaction of this demand decreases the supplies of foreign monies held by American banks
   B. foreign demand for dollars and the satisfaction of this demand increases the supplies of foreign monies held by American banks
   C. American demand for foreign monies and the satisfaction of this demand decreases the supplies of foreign monies held by American banks
   D. American demand for foreign monies and the satisfaction of this demand increases the supplies of dollars held by foreign banks

18. If an American importer can purchase 10,000 pounds for $20,000, the rate of exchange is

   A. $1=2 pounds in the United States
   B. $2=1 pound in the United States
   C. $1=2 pounds in Great Britain
   D. $.5=1 pound in Great Britain

19. Which of the following creates a supply of Italian lira in foreign exchange markets? A(n)

   A. Frenchman redeems a bond issued by an Italian manufacturer
   B. Italian exporter buys insurance from an American firm
   C. American student takes a summer trip to Rome
   D. American importer buys 500 cases of Italian table wine

20. If the dollar price of yen rises, then

   A. the yen price of dollars also rises
   B. the dollar depreciates relative to the yen
   C. the yen depreciates relative to the dollar
   D. all of the above will occur

21. Monopolistic competition means

   A. a market situation where competition is based entirely on product differentiation and advertising
   B. a large number of firms producing a standardized or homogeneous product
   C. many firms producing differentiated products
   D. a few firms producing a standardized or homogeneous product

22. Under monopolistic competition, entry to the industry is 22.____

    A. completely free of barriers
    B. more difficult than under pure competition but not nearly as difficult as under pure monopoly
    C. more difficult than under pure monopoly
    D. blocked

23. Nonprice competition refers to 23.____

    A. competition between products of different industries, for example, competition between aluminum and steel in the manufacture of automobile parts
    B. price increases by a firm which are ignored by its rivals
    C. advertising, product promotion, and changes in the real or perceived characteristics of a product
    D. reductions in production costs which are not reflected in price reductions

24. The book publishing, furniture, and clothing industries are each illustrations of 24.____

    A. countervailing power
    B. homogeneous oligopoly
    C. monopolistic competition
    D. pure monopoly

25. If the number of firms in a monopolistically competitive industry increases and the degree of product differentiation diminishes, 25.____

    A. the likelihood of realizing economic profits in the long run would be enhanced
    B. individual firms would now be operating at outputs where their average total costs would be higher
    C. the industry would more closely approximate pure competition
    D. the likelihood of collusive pricing would increase

KEY (CORRECT ANSWERS)

1. B
2. B
3. C
4. D
5. C

6. C
7. D
8. A
9. B
10. B

11. C
12. A
13. B
14. C
15. D

16. D
17. D
18. B
19. B
20. B

21. C
22. B
23. C
24. C
25. C

TEST 3

DIRECTIONS: Each question or incomplete statement is followed by several suggested answers or completions. Select the one that BEST answers the question or completes the Statement. *PRINT THE LETTER OF THE CORRECT ANSWER IN THE SPACE AT THE RIGHT.*

1. The term *oligopoly* indicates 1.____

   A. a one-firm industry
   B. many producers of a differentiated product
   C. a few firms producing either a differentiated or a homogeneous product
   D. an industry whose four-firm concentration ratio is low

2. In an oligopolistic market, 2.____

   A. one firm is always dominant
   B. products may be standardized or differentiated
   C. the four largest firms account for 20 percent of total sales
   D. the industry is monopolistically competitive

3. Oligopolistic industries are characterized by a 3.____

   A. few dominant firms ane substantial entry barriers
   B. few dominant firms and no barriers to entry
   C. large number of firms and low entry barriers
   D. few dominant firms and low entry barriers

4. The automobile, household appliance, and automobile tire industries are all illustrations of 4.____

   A. homogeneous oligopoly   B. monopolistic competition
   C. pure monopoly   D. differentiated oligopoly

5. Barriers to entry in oligopolistic industries may consist of 5.____

   A. economies of scale
   B. patents
   C. ownership of essential resources
   D. all of the above

6. Which of the following industries is an illustration of homogeneous oligopoly? 6.____

   A. Household laundry equipment
   B. Cigarettes
   C. Aluminum
   D. The beer industry

7. If an industry evolves from monopolistic competition to oligopoly, we would expect 7.____

   A. the four-firm concentration ratio to decrease
   B. the four-firm concentration ratio to increase
   C. the four-firm concentration ratio might either increase or decrease
   D. that barriers to entry have weakened

8. One would expect that collusion among oligopolistic producers would be easiest to achieve in a _____ firms producing a _____ product.

   A. rather large number of; differentiated
   B. very few; differentiated
   C. rather large number of; homogeneous
   D. very few; homogeneous

9. Historically, when the new models of automobiles were put on the market each fall, General Motors would establish prices for each of its basic models. Ford and Chrysler would then set the prices of comparable models within a few dollars of GM's prices. This describes

   A. shadow pricing
   B. a cartel
   C. markup pricing
   D. price leadership

10. The main purpose of the antitrust laws is

    A. to encourage firms to produce where P > MC
    B. the elimination of both negative and positive externalities
    C. to prevent the monopolization of industries
    D. to regulate natural monopolies

11. Responsibility for enforcing the antitrust laws rests

    A. with the Interstate Commerce Commission
    B. with both the Department of Justice and the Federal Trade Commission
    C. solely with the Federal Trade Commission
    D. solely with the Department of Justice

12. The Sherman Act

    A. was declared unconstitutional in 1895
    B. provided for government regulation of the railroads
    C. declared monopoly and restraints of trade to be illegal
    D. exempted the railroad and communications industries from the antitrust laws

13. Federal legislation and policies

    A. consistently promote competition
    B. consistently inhibit competition
    C. sometimes promote and sometimes inhibit competition
    D. have no significant impact upon the competitiveness of industry

14. Tying agreements

    A. establish common boards of directors for previously competing firms
    B. obligate a purchaser of product X to also buy product Y from the same seller
    C. allow manufacturers to specify the retail prices of their products
    D. prohibit firms from selling their products outside of specified geographic areas

15. Price fixing

    A. is prohibited by Section 7 of the Clayton Act
    B. is a per se violation of the antitrust laws
    C. may be either legal or illegal depending on whether or not it produces above-normal profits
    D. is illegal under terms of the Federal Trade Commission Act

16. Price fixing is considered to be a per se violation of the antitrust laws because

    A. a guilty verdict requires proof of injury to consumers
    B. a guilty verdict requires proof of injury to other competitors
    C. the rule of reason is applicable
    D. a guilty verdict requires proof that the activity was attempted, not that it unreasonably restrained trade

17. The *rule of reason* indicated that

    A. if less than four firms account for three-fourths of an industry's sales, the industry is in violation of the Sherman Act
    B. social regulation should not be enforced unreasonably so that costs exceed benefits
    C. the mere possession of monopoly power is a violation of the antitrust laws
    D. only contracts and combinations which *unreasonably* restrain trade violate the antitrust laws

18. In the United States Steel case of 1920, the courts held that

    A. the structure of an industry is more important than its behavior in determining violations of the antitrust laws
    B. any firm which faces substantial import competition is exempt from the antitrust laws
    C. although United States Steel possessed monopoly power, it had not violated the Sherman Act because it had not unreasonably used that power
    D. the fact that United States Steel possessed monopoly power was a violation of the Sherman Act

19. The basic issue in the duPont cellophane case was

    A. whether trade crossed state lines
    B. defining the relevant market
    C. structure versus behavior
    D. the rule of reason

20. A firm charged with monopolizing a market is less likely to be convicted if

    A. the court accepts a broad definition of the market
    B. the court accepts a narrow definition of the market
    C. it has gained its monopoly through abusive means
    D. it sells its product to other firms, rather than directly to consumers

21. Restructuring of a major industry resulted from the

    A. United States Steel case
    B. AT&T case
    C. IBM case
    D. duPont cellophane case

22. A vertical merger involves a combining of one or more firms

    A. as the result of one firm purchasing the assets of the other
    B. that are operating in entirely different industries
    C. operating at different stages of the production process in a particular industry
    D. operating at the same stage of the production process

23. A merger between an automobile manufacturer and a maker of automobile tires is an example of a

    A. conglomerate merger   B. horizontal merger
    C. vertical merger   D. tying contract

24. A merger of several firms operating in different industries – for example, a trucking company, a fast-food chain, and a brokerage house – is called a(n) _____ merger.

    A. integrated   B. conglomerate
    C. vertical   D. horizontal

25. Which of the following is CORRECT?

    A. Vertical mergers are more likely to be acceptable under antitrust laws than are horizontal mergers.
    B. A vertical merger entails the merging of two or more competing firms.
    C. Horizontal mergers are more likely to be acceptable under antitrust laws than are vertical mergers.
    D. Conglomerate mergers occur when two or more firms at various stages in a good's production are combined.

26. Which one of the following is NOT correct?

    A. In antitrust cases, defendants attempt to define the relevant market broadly.
    B. The courts have varied over time in their interpretations of the antitrust statutes.
    C. Antitrust suits can only be originated by the Federal Trade Commission.
    D. In antitrust cases, the prosecution attempts to define the relevant market narrowly.

Questions 27-28.

DIRECTIONS: Questions 27 and 28 are to be answered on the basis of the following table showing market shares of firms in hypothetical industries. Assume these are distinct industries with no buyer-seller relationships or competition among them.

	Market Share of Firms in Industry					
Industry	1	2	3	4	5	6
Alpha	30	30	20	20	--	--
Beta	80	10	5	3	1	1
Cappa	25	25	25	25	--	--
Delta	20	20	20	20	10	10

27. The Herfindahl Index for Cappa is   27.____

    A. 2500   B. 100   C. 100,000   D. 5,000

28. The government would likely challenge a merger between   28.____

    A. Firm 1 in Alpha and Firm 6 in Delta
    B. Firms 3 and 4 in Beta
    C. Firms 1 and 2 in Cappa
    D. Firm 4 in Alpha and Firm 3 in Cappa

29. A firm is likely to be a natural monopoly   29.____

    A. when the demand for its product or service is inelastic
    B. if it is producing an inferior good
    C. if economies of scale are experienced over the full range of output
    D. because government grants it an exclusive franchise

30. Using antitrust law to split up an unregulated natural monopoly into several competing   30.____
    firms

    A. would reduce product price
    B. would increase product price
    C. might either increase product price or reduce product price
    D. will reduce average total cost.

KEY (CORRECT ANSWERS)

1.	C	16.	D
2.	C	17.	D
3.	A	18.	C
4.	D	19.	B
5.	D	20.	A
6.	C	21.	B
7.	B	22.	C
8.	D	23.	C
9.	D	24.	B
10.	C	25.	A
11.	B	26.	C
12.	C	27.	A
13.	C	28.	C
14.	B	29.	C
15.	B	30.	B

EXAMINATION SECTION
TEST 1

DIRECTIONS: Each question or incomplete statement is followed by several suggested answers or completions. Select the one that BEST answers the question or completes the statement. *PRINT THE LETTER OF THE CORRECT ANSWER IN THE SPACE AT THE RIGHT.*

Questions 1-4.

DIRECTIONS: Questions 1 through 4 are to be answered on the basis of the diagram below.

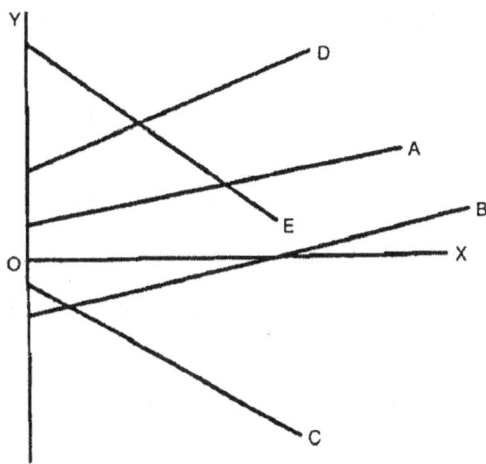

1. Which line(s) show(s) a positive relationship between x and y?

   A. A *only*
   C. A, B, and D
   B. Both A and D
   D. Both C and E

   1.____

2. Which line(s) show(s) a negative relationship between x and y?

   A. A *only*
   C. A, B, and D
   B. Both A and D
   D. Both C and E

   2.____

3. Which line(s) show(s) a positive vertical intercept?

   A. A and D *only*
   C. A, D, and E
   B. B and C *only*
   D. A, D, and B

   3.____

4. Which line(s) show(s) a negative vertical intercept?

   A. C *only*
   C. B, C, and E
   B. Both C and E
   D. Both B and C

   4.____

Questions 5-7.

DIRECTIONS: Questions 5 through 7 are to be answered on the basis of the following diagram.

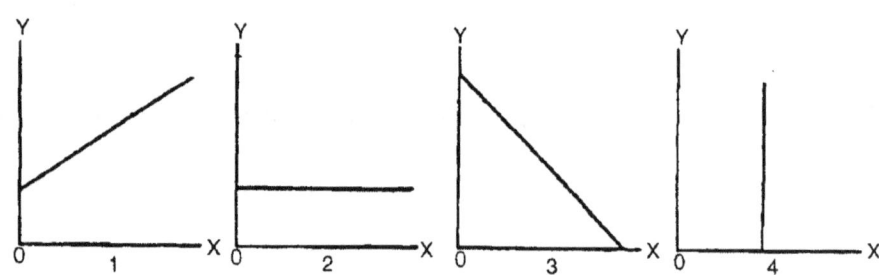

5. The amount of Y is directly related to the amount of X in

   A. both 1 and 3
   B. both 1 and 2
   C. 2 only
   D. 1 only

6. The amount of Y is inversely related to the amount of X in

   A. 2 only
   B. both 1 and 3
   C. 3 only
   D. 1 only

7. The amount of Y is unrelated to the amount of X in

   A. both 2 and 4
   B. 3 only
   C. 2 only
   D. 1 only

8.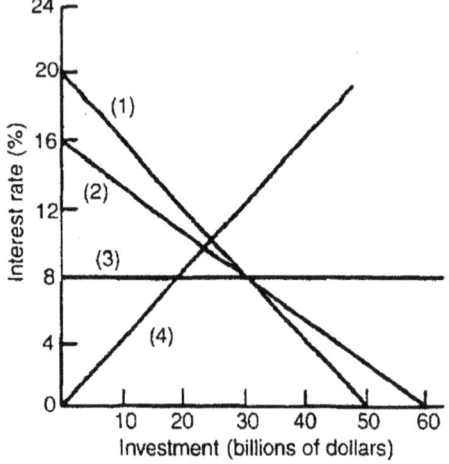

Assume that if the interest rate which businesses must pay to borrow funds were 20 percent, it would be unprofitable for businesses to invest in new machinery and equipment so that investment would be zero. But if the interest rate were 16 percent, businesses will find it profitable to invest $10 billion. If the interest rate were 12 percent, $20 billion would be invested. Assume that total investment continues to increase by $10 billion for each successive 4 percentage point decline in the interest rate. Refer to the above graph. Which of the following is the correct graphical presentation of the indicated relationship? Line

A. 4   B. 3   C. 2   D. 1

Questions 9-11.

DIRECTIONS: Questions 9 through 11 are to be answered on the basis of the following data.

After-tax Income	Consumption
$1,000	$ 900
2,000	1,800
3,000	2,700
4,000	3,600
5,000	4,500

9. The above data suggest that

   A. consumption varies inversely with after-tax income
   B. consumption varies directly with after-tax income
   C. consumption and after-tax income are unrelated
   D. a tax increase will increase consumption

9.____

10. The above data indicate that

    A. consumers spend 80 percent of their after-tax incomes
    B. consumers spend 90 percent of their after-tax incomes
    C. a tax reduction will reduce consumption
    D. the relationship between consumption and after-tax income is random

10.____

11. The above data suggest that

    A. a policy of tax reduction will increase consumption
    B. a policy of tax increases will increase consumption
    C. tax changes will have no impact upon consumption
    D. after-tax income should be lowered in order to increase consumption

11.____

Questions 12-15.

DIRECTIONS: Questions 12 through 15 are to be answered on the basis of the following diagram.

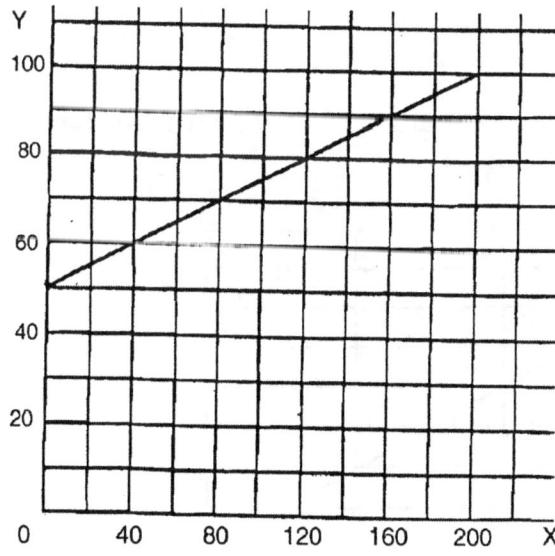

12. The variables X and Y are

    A. inversely related
    B. directly related
    C. unrelated
    D. negatively related

13. The vertical intercept

    A. is 40
    B. is 50
    C. is 60
    D. cannot be determined from the information given

14. The slope of the line

    A. is -1/4
    B. is +1/4
    C. is .40
    D. cannot be determined from the information given

15. The equation which shows the relationship between Y and X is

    A. Y = 50 + 1/4 X
    B. X = 1/4 Y
    C. Y = 4X
    D. Y = 1/4 X - 50

16. The movement from line A to line A' represents a change in

    A. the slope *only*
    B. the intercept *only*
    C. both the slope and the intercept
    D. neither the slope nor the intercept

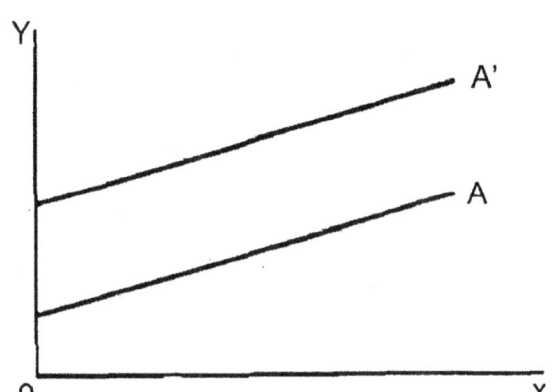

Questions 17-19.

DIRECTIONS: Questions 17 through 19 are to be answered on the basis of the following graph.

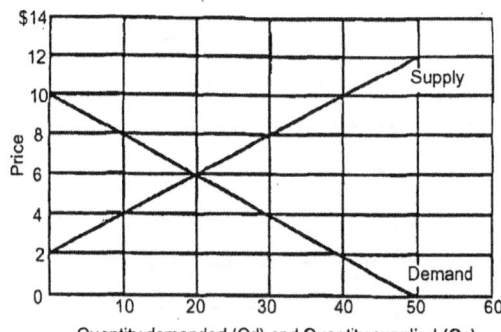

17. Which of the following statements is CORRECT 17.____

    A. Quantity demanded and quantity supplied are independent of price.
    B. Price and quantity demanded are directly related.
    C. Price and quantity supplied are directly related.
    D. Price and quantity supplied are inversely related.

18. Which of the following schedules correctly reflects *demand*? 18.____

A		B		C		D	
P	Qd	P	Qd	P	Qd	P	Qd
$12	0	$14	0	$14	60	$12	0
10	0	12	0	12	50	10	10
8	10	10	20	10	40-	8	20
6	20	8	40	8	30	6	30
4	30	6	60	6	20	4	40
2	40	4	80	4	10	2	50

19. Which of the following schedules correctly reflects *supply*? 19.____

A		B		C		D	
P	Qs	P	Qs	P	Qs	P	Qs
$12	50	$14	50	$12	50	$12	0
10	30	12	40	10	40	10	0
8	10	10	30	8	30	8	10
6	0	8	20	6	20	6	20
4	0	6	10	4	10	4	30
2	0	4	0	2	0	2	40

Questions 20-22.

DIRECTIONS: Questions 20 through 22 are to be answered on the basis of the following diagram.

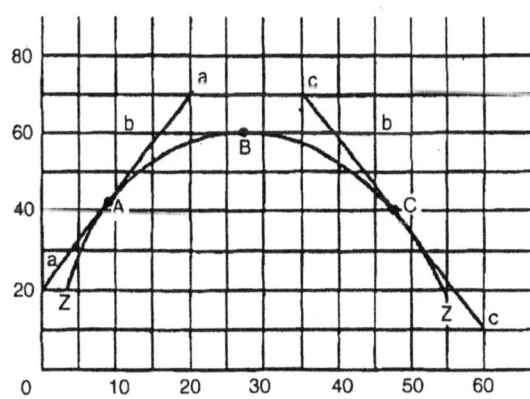

20. The slope of curve ZZ at point A is

    A. +2
    B. +2 1/2
    C. -2 1/2
    D. +4
    E. none of the above

21. The slope of curve ZZ at point B is

    A. infinity
    B. zero
    C. one
    D. none of the above

22. The slope of curve ZZ at point C is

    A. -4
    B. -2
    C. -2 2/5
    D. +3
    E. none of the above

23. Slopes of lines are especially important in economics because

    A. they measure marginal changes
    B. they always tell us something about profits
    C. positive slopes are always preferred to negative slopes
    D. they always relate to resource and output scarcity

24. The slope of a straight line can be determined by

    A. comparing the absolute horizontal change to the absolute vertical change between two points on the line
    B. comparing the absolute vertical change to the absolute horizontal change between two points on the line
    C. taking the reciprocal of the vertical intercept
    D. comparing the percentage vertical change to the percentage horizontal change between two points on the line

25. The measured slope of a line

    A. is independent of how the two variables are denominated
    B. will be affected by how the two variables are denominated
    C. necessarily diminishes as one moves rightward on the line
    D. necessarily increases as one moves rightward on the line

KEY (CORRECT ANSWERS)

1.	C	11.	A
2.	D	12.	B
3.	C	13.	B
4.	D	14.	B
5.	D	15.	A
6.	C	16.	B
7.	A	17.	C
8.	D	18.	A
9.	B	19.	C
10.	B	20.	A

21. A
22. B
23. A
24. B
25. B

TEST 2

DIRECTIONS: Each question or incomplete statement is followed by several suggested answers or completions. Select the one that BEST answers the question or completes the statement. *PRINT THE LETTER OF THE CORRECT ANSWER IN THE SPACE AT THE RIGHT.*

Questions 1-3.

DIRECTIONS: Questions 1 through 3 are to be answered on the basis of the given supply and demand data for wheat.

Bushels Demanded Per Month	Price Per Bushel	Bushels Supplied Per Month
45	$5	77
50	4	73
56	3	68
61	2	61
67	1	57

1. Equilibrium price will be

    A. $4   B. $3   C. $2   D. $1

2. If the price in this market was $4,

    A. farmers would reduce the number of acres allocated to the growing of wheat
    B. buyers would want to purchase more wheat than is currently being supplied
    C. farmers would not be able to sell all of their wheat
    D. there would be a shortage of wheat

3. If price was initially $4, we would expect

    A. quantity supplied to continue to exceed quantity demanded
    B. the quantity of wheat supplied to decline as a result of the subsequent price change
    C. the quantity of wheat demanded to fall as a result of the subsequent price change
    D. the price of wheat to rise

1.____

2.____

3.____

Questions 4-6.

DIRECTIONS: Questions 4 through 6 are to be answered on the basis of the following diagram.

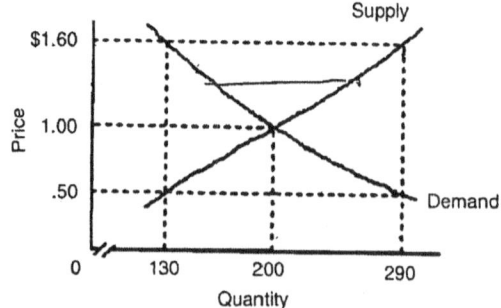

98

4. The equilibrium price and quantity in this market will be   4._____

   A. $1.00 and 130   B. $1.00 and 200
   C. $1.60 and 130   D. $.50 and 130

5. A surplus of 160 units would be encountered if price was   5._____

   A. $1.10, that is, $1.60 minus $.50
   B. $1.60
   C. $1.00
   D. $.50

6. A shortage of 160 units would be encountered if price was   6._____

   A. $1.10, that is, $1.60 minus $.50
   B. $1.60
   C. $1.00
   D. $.50

Questions 7-10.

DIRECTIONS: Questions 7 through 10 are to be answered on the basis of the following diagram.

7. A price of $60 in this market will result in a _____ of _____ units.   7._____

   A. shortage; 50   B. surplus; 50
   C. surplus; 100   D. shortage; 100

8. A price of $20 in this market will result in a _____ of _____ units.   8._____

   A. shortage; 50   B. surplus; 50
   C. surplus; 100   D. shortage; 100

9. The highest price that buyers will be willing and able to pay for 100 units of this product is   9._____

   A. $30   B. $60   C. $40   D. $20

10. If this is a competitive market, price and quantity will gravitate toward _____, respectively.   10._____

    A. $60 and 100   B. $60 and 200
    C. $40 and 150   D. $20 and 150

Questions 11-16.

DIRECTIONS: Questions 11 through 16 are to be answered on the basis of the following diagrams.

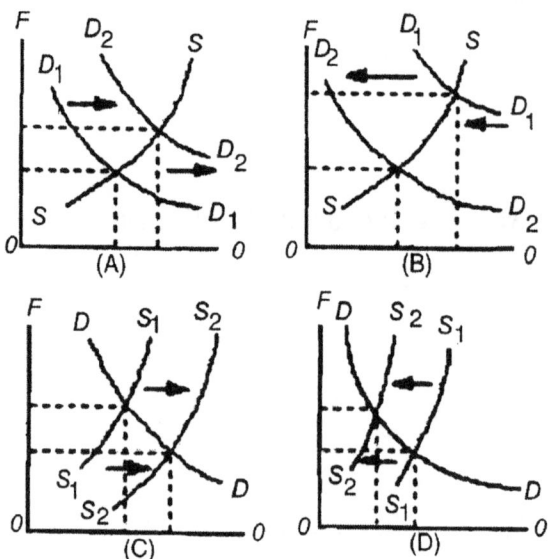

11. Which of the above diagrams illustrate(s) the effect of an increase in automobile worker wages on the market for automobiles?

    A. A   B. B   C. C   D. D

12. Which of the above diagrams illustrate(s) the effect of a decline in the price of personal computers upon the market for software?

    A. A only   B. A and D   C. B only   D. D only

13. Which of the above diagrams illustrate(s) the effect of an increase in the price of Budweiser upon the market for Coors?

    A. A   B. B   C. C   D. D

14. Which of the above diagrams illustrate(s) the effect of a decrease in incomes upon the market for secondhand clothing?

    A. A   B. B   C. C   D. D

15. Which of the above diagrams illustrate(s) the effect of a governmental subsidy on the market for AIDS research?

    A. A   B. B   C. C   D. D

16. Which of the above diagrams illustrate(s) the effect of a decline in the price of irrigation equipment upon the market for corn?

    A. A   B. B   C. C   D. D

Questions 17-21.

DIRECTIONS: Questions 17 through 21 are to be answered on the basis of the following cost data for a competitive seller.

Total Product	Total Fixed Cost	Total Variable Cost	Total Cost
0	$50	$ 0	$ 0
1	50	70	120
2	50	120	170
3	50	150	200
4	50	220	270
5	50	300	350
6	50	390	440

17. The above data are for

   A. the long run
   B. the short run
   C. both the short run and the long run
   D. the intermediate market period only

18. At 5 units of output average fixed cost, average variable cost, and average total cost are _____, respectively.

   A. $10, $60, and $70
   B. $50, $40, and $90
   C. $10, $70, and $80
   D. $5, $25, and $30

19. The marginal cost of the fifth unit of output

   A. is $80
   B. is $90
   C. is $50
   D. cannot be determined from the information given

20. If product price is $75, the firm will produce _____ units of output.

   A. 3   B. 4   C. 5   D. 6

21. Given the $75 product price, at its optimal output the firm will realize a

   A. $25 economic profit
   B. $30 economic profit
   C. $25 loss
   D. $30 loss

Questions 22-24.

DIRECTIONS: Questions 22 through 24 are to be answered on the basis of the following short-run data.

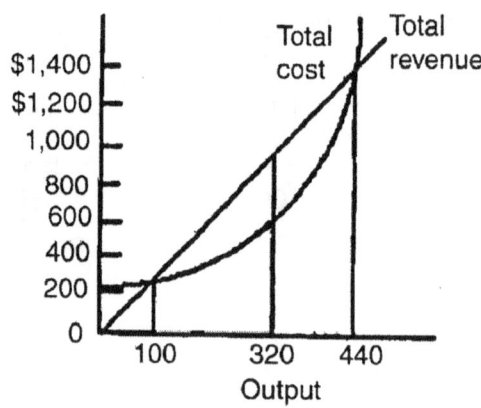

22. The total fixed cost for this firm is

 A. about $67 B. $300 C. $200 D. $100

23. The shape of the total cost curve reflects

 A. diminishing opportunity costs
 B. the law of rising fixed costs
 C. increasing and diminishing returns
 D. economies and diseconomies of scale

24. The profit-maximizing output for this firm is _____ units.

 A. above 440 B. 440 C. 320 D. 100

25. A competitive firm will maximize profits at that output at which

 A. the excess of total revenue over total cost is greatest
 B. total revenue and total cost are equal
 C. price exceeds average total cost by the largest amount
 D. the difference between marginal revenue and price is at a maximum

KEY (CORRECT ANSWERS)

1. C
2. C
3. B
4. B
5. B

6. D
7. C
8. D
9. B
10. C

11. D
12. A
13. A
14. A
15. C

16. C
17. B
18. A
19. A
20. B

21. B
22. C
23. C
24. B
25. A

TEST 3

DIRECTIONS: Each question or incomplete statement is followed by several suggested answers or completions. Select the one that BEST answers the question or completes the statement. *PRINT THE LETTER OF THE CORRECT ANSWER IN THE SPACE AT THE RIGHT.*

1. Which of the following statements is CORRECT? 1.____

    A. The value of the independent variable is determined by the value of the dependent variable.
    B. The value of the dependent variable is determined by the value of the independent variable.
    C. The dependent variable designates the *cause* and the independent variable the *effect*.
    D. Dependent variables graph as upsloping lines; independent variables graph as downsloping lines.

Questions 2-4.

DIRECTIONS: Questions 2 through 4 are to be answered on the basis of the following cost data for a purely competitive seller.

Output	Total Cost
0	$ 50
1	90
2	120
3	140
4	170
5	210
6	260
7	330

2. If product price is $60, the firm will 2.____

    A. close down
    B. produce 4 units and realize a $120 profit
    C. produce 6 units and realize a $100 profit
    D. produce 3 units and realize a $40 loss

3. If product price is $45, the firm will 3.____

    A. close down
    B. produce 4 units and realize a $120 economic profit
    C. produce 5 units and realize a $15 economic profit
    D. produce 6 units and realize a $100 economic profit

4. If product price is $25, the firm will 4.____

    A. close down and realize a $90 loss
    B. close down and realize a $50 loss
    C. produce 3 units and realize a $65 loss
    D. produce 4 units and realize a $10 economic profit

Questions 5-6.

DIRECTIONS: Questions 5 and 6 are to be answered on the basis of the following diagrams.

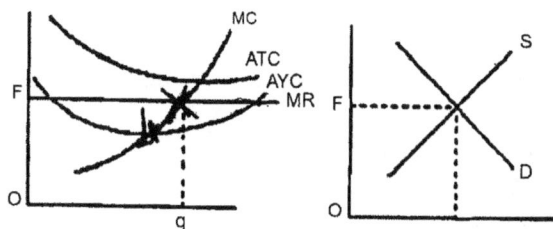

5. Referring to the above diagrams, which pertain to a purely competitive firm producing output Oq and the industry in which it operates, in the long run we should expect

    A. firms to enter the industry, market supply to rise, and product price to fall
    B. firms to leave the industry, market supply to rise, and product price to fall
    C. firms to leave the industry, market supply to fall, and product price to rise
    D. no change in the number of firms in this industry

5._____

6. Referring to the above diagrams, which pertain to a purely competitive firm producing output Oq and the industry in which it operates, the predicted long-run adjustments in this industry might be offset by

    A. a decline in product demand
    B. an increase in resource prices
    C. a technological improvement in production methods
    D. none of the above

6._____

Questions 7-8.

DIRECTIONS: Questions 7 and 8 are to be answered on the basis of the following diagram.

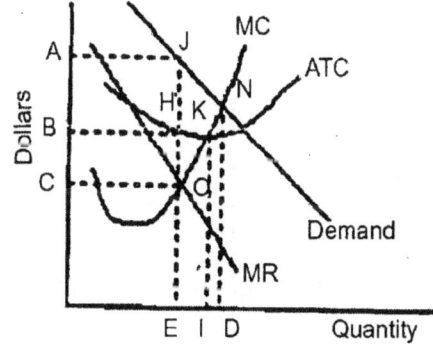

7. In order to maximize profits or minimize losses, this firm should produce _____ units and charge price _____.

    A. OE; OC   B. OE; OA   C. OM; NM   D. OL; LK

7._____

105

8. In equilibrium, total revenue will be

   A. NM times OM
   B. OAJE
   C. OEGC
   D. OEHB

Questions 9-13.

DIRECTIONS: Questions 9 through 13 are to be answered on the basis of the following list.

   A. Monopolistic competition
   B. Oligopoly
   C. Pure monopoly
   D. Pure competition

9. An industry comprised of 40 firms, none of which has more than 3 percent of the total market for a differentiated product.

10. A one-firm industry.

11. An industry comprised of four firms, each of which has approximately 25 percent of the total market for a product.

12. An industry comprised of a very large number of sellers which are producing a standardized product.

13. An industry comprised of a small number of firms, each of which considers the potential reactions of its rivals in making price-output decisions.

Questions 14-15.

DIRECTIONS: Questions 14 and 15 are to be answered on the basis of the information given in the following table.

Employment	Total Product	Product Price
0	0	$3
1	12	3
2	22	3
3	30	3
4	36	3
5	40	3
6	42	3

14. If the firm is hiring workers under purely competitive conditions at a wage rate of $22, it will choose to employ _____ worker(s).

   A. 1   B. 2   C. 3   D. 4

15. If the firm is hiring workers under purely competitive conditions at a wage rate of $10, it will choose to employ _____ workers.

   A. 2   B. 3   C. 4   D. 5

16. The MRP curve for labor

    A. is downsloping and shows the relationship between wage rates and the quantity of labor demanded
    B. is perfectly elastic if the firm is selling its output competitively
    C. is upsloping and lies above the labor supply curve
    D. will shift location when the wage rate changes

Questions 17-19.

DIRECTIONS: Questions 17 through 19 are to be answered on the basis of the following information.

A farmer who has fixed amounts of land and capital finds that total product is 24 for the first worker hired; 32 when two workers are hired; 37 when three are hired; and 40 when four are hired. The farmer's product sells for $3 per unit and the wage rate is $13 per worker.

17. The marginal product of the second worker

    A. is 24   B. is 8   C. is 5
    D. cannot be determined from the information given

18. The marginal revenue product of the second worker is

    A. $24   B. $8   C. $15   D. $9

19. How many workers should the farmer hire?

    A. 1   B. 2   C. 3   D. 4

20. A competitive employer is using labor in such an amount that labor's MRP is $10 and its wage rate is $8. We can conclude that the firm

    A. should hire more labor because this will increase profits
    B. should hire more labor, although this may either increase or decrease profits
    C. is currently hiring the profit-maximizing amount of labor
    D. none of the above

21.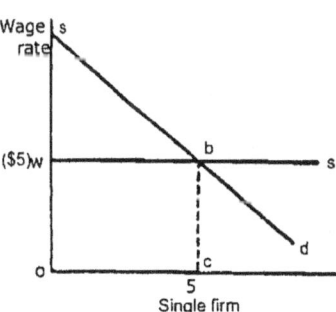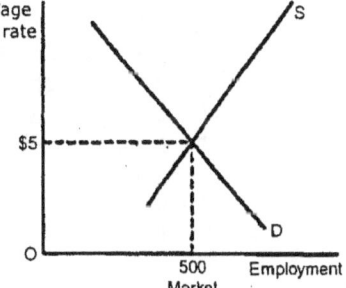

Referring to the above diagrams, the firm

    A. is a monopsonist in the hire of labor
    B. must be selling its product in an imperfectly competitive market
    C. is a *wage taker*
    D. must pay a higher marginal resource cost for each successive worker

22.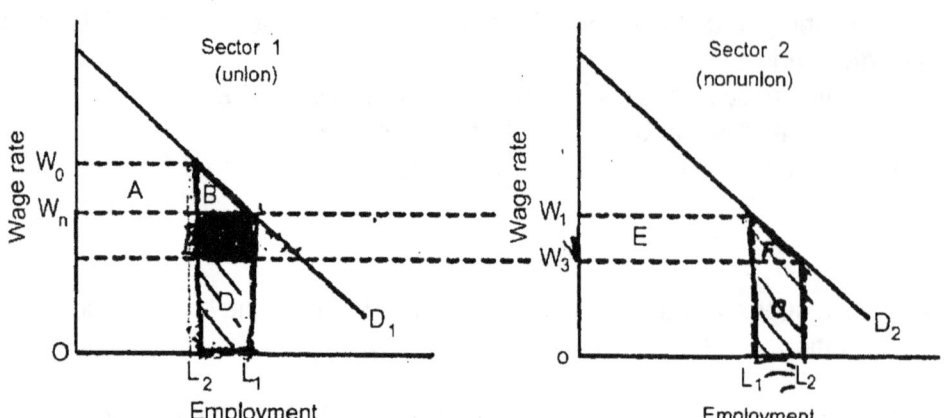

Referring to the above diagrams which show two sectors of the labor market for a particular kind of labor, relevant product markets are assumed to be competitive. The two labor demand curves are identical, and initially the quantities of labor employed in the two sectors are L_1 and L'_1 and the wage rate in each sector is Wn. This analysis suggests that the union wage advantage causes a net efficiency

A. loss equal to E-A
B. loss equal to C
C. gain equal to C
D. gain equal to B

23. Critics of unions argue that unions diminish efficiency and productivity by

A. engaging in featherbedding
B. precipitating strikes
C. causing a misallocation of labor
D. all of the above

Questions 24-25.

DIRECTIONS: Questions 24 and 25 are to be answered on the basis of the following diagrams.

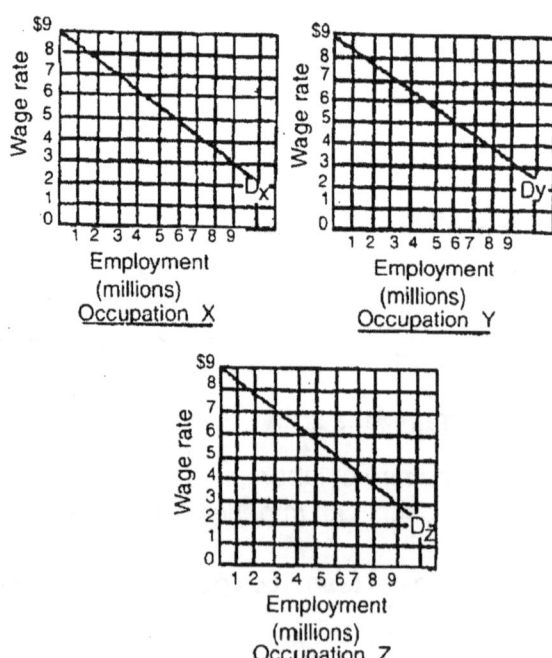

24. It is assumed that (1) the labor force is comprised of 9 million male and 9 million female workers; (2) the economy is comprised of 3 occupations, X, Y, and Z, each having identical demand curves for labor; (3) male and female workers are homogeneous with respect to their labor-market capabilities; (4) women are discriminated against in that they are excluded from occupations X and Y and are confined to Z; and (5) aside from discrimination, the economy is otherwise competitive. Under these circumstances, 9 million women will be employed in occupation Z

    A. 5 million men in X, and 4 million men in Y
    B. 3 million men in X, and 6 million men in Y
    C. 6 million men in X, and 3 million men in Y
    D. and 4 1/2 million men each in occupations X and Y

25. It is assumed that (1) the labor force is comprised of 9 million male and 9 million female workers; (2) the economy is comprised of 3 occupations, X, Y, and Z, each having identical demand curves for labor; (3) male and female workers are homogeneous with respect to their labor-market capabilities; (4) women are discriminated against in that they are excluded from occupations X and Y and are confined to Z; and (5) aside from discrimination, the economy is otherwise competitive. The elimination of gender discrimination

    A. may either increase or reduce real domestic output, depending upon what happens to the level of nominal wages
    B. will increase real domestic output
    C. will have no effect on real domestic output
    D. will reduce real domestic output

26. As applied to gender discrimination, the crowding model of occupational-segregation
    A. helps explain why women earn less than men
    B. predicts that men's wages would fall and women's wages would rise if occupational segregation was eliminated
    C. predicts that the domestic output would increase if occupational segregation was ended
    D. all of the above

Questions 27-29.

DIRECTIONS: Questions 27 through 29 are to be answered on the basis of the following figures.

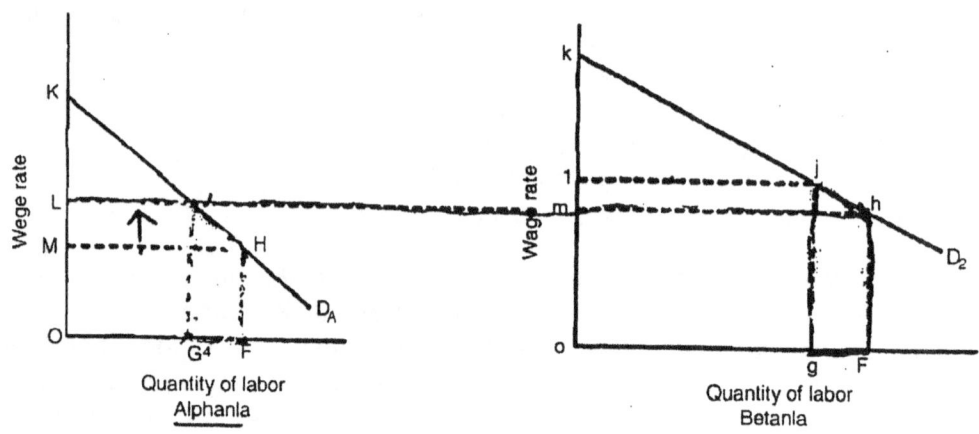

27. It is assumed that (a) the demands for labor in Alphania and Betania are as shown by D_A and D_B, respectively; (b) Alphania's native labor force is OF and that of Betania is Og; and (c) full employment exists in both countries. If migration is costless and unimpeded,

    A. migration will cause the average level of wages to fall in Alphania
    B. no migration will occur
    C. fg workers will move from Betania to Alphania
    D. GF workers will move from Alphania to Betania

28. It is assumed that (a) the demands for labor in Alphania and Betania are as shown by D_A and D_B, respectively; (b) Alphania's native labor force is OF and that of Betania is Og; and (c) full employment exists in both countries. If migration is costless and unimpeded, the average level of wages will

    A. decrease in Betania, but remain unchanged in Alphania
    B. increase in Alphania, but remain unchanged in Betania
    C. increase in Alphania and decrease in Betania
    D. increase in Betania and decrease in Alphania

29. It is assumed that (a) the demands for labor in Alphania and Betania are as shown by D_A and D_B, respectively; (b) Alphania's native labor force is OF and that of Betania is Og; and (c) full employment exists in both countries. After migration has ceased,

    A. world output will have increased by mljh-MLJH
    B. Betania's output will have increased and Alphania's output will have decreased, but world output will not have changed
    C. world output will have increased by gjhf-GJHF
    D. world output will have decreased by gjhf-GJHF

30. Voluntary migration of skilled craftworkers from low-paying to high-paying nations is most likely to be opposed by 30._____

    A. business groups in the high-paying nations
    B. craft workers who stay in the low-paying nations
    C. industrial unions in the high-paying nations
    D. craft unions in the high-paying nations

KEY (CORRECT ANSWERS)

1.	B	16.	A
2.	C	17.	B
3.	C	18.	A
4.	B	19.	C
5.	D	20.	A
6.	C	21.	C
7.	A	22.	B
8.	A	23.	D
9.	A	24.	D
10.	C	25.	B
11.	B	26.	D
12.	D	27.	D
13.	B	28.	C
14.	C	29.	C
15.	D	30.	D

www.ingramcontent.com/pod-product-compliance
Lightning Source LLC
Chambersburg PA
CBHW082149300426
44117CB00016B/2662